WALKING IN THE CANARY ISLANDS: VOLUME 2 EAST

GRAN CANARIA, FUERTEVENTURA, LANZAROTE AND GRACIOSA

ABOUT THE AUTHOR

Paddy Dillon is a prolific outdoor writer with a score and more books to his name, as well as a dozen booklets and brochures. He writes for a number of outdoor magazines and other publications, as well as producing materials for tourism groups and other organisations. He lives on the fringe of the Lake District, and has walked, and written about walking, in every county in England, Scotland, Ireland and Wales. He generally leads at least one guided walking holiday overseas every year and has walked in many parts of Europe, as well as Nepal, Tibet and the Canadian Rockies.

While walking his routes, Paddy inputs his notes directly into a palmtop computer every few steps. His descriptions are therefore precise, having been written at the very point at which the reader uses them. He takes all his own photographs and often draws his own maps to illustrate his routes. He has appeared on television, and is a member of the Outdoor Writers' Guild.

Cicerone guides by Paddy Dillon:

Irish Coastal Walks
The Irish Coast to Coast
The Mountains of Ireland
Channel Island Walks
The Isles of Scilly
Walking in the Isle of Arran

Walking the Galloway Hills
Walking in County Durham
Walking the North Pennines
GR20 Corsica: High Level Route
Walking in Madeira
Walking in the Canaries: Vol 1 West

WALKING IN THE CANARY ISLANDS: VOLUME 2 EAST

GRAN CANARIA, FUERTEVENTURA, LANZAROTE AND GRACIOSA

By
Paddy Dillon

CICERONE

2 POLICE SQUARE, MILNTHORPE, CUMBRIA LA7 7PY
www.cicerone.co.uk

© Paddy Dillon 2002

ISBN 1 85284 368 3

A catalogue record for this book is available from the British Library.

Photographs by the author.

Advice to Readers

Readers are advised that while every effort is taken by the author to ensure the accuracy of this guidebook, changes can occur which may affect the contents. It is advisable to check locally on transport, accommodation, shops, etc, but even rights of way can be altered.

The publisher would welcome notes of any such changes.

Front cover: Walking away from the Roque Nublo, a sacred site to the ancient Guanches, on Gran Canaria (Walk 5)

CONTENTS

Map of the Canary Islands 9

Introduction 11
Location 11
Geology...11
Discovery and History 12
Weather...14
Landscape 15
Language 16
Island Trees and Flowers..18
Island Birds...20
Island Animals 20
National Parks and Protected Areas 22
Getting to the Canary Islands...22
Getting Around the Canary Islands 24
Accommodation..26
Tourist Information 27
Maps of the Canary Islands..27
The Plan of this Guide...28
Emergency Assistance..29

Gran Canaria..31
Walk 1   Dunas de Maspalomas 34
Walk 2   Arteara to Palmitos Park 36
Walk 3   Cruz Grande to Palmitos Park 40
Walk 4   San Bartolomé Circuit...44
Walk 5   Roque Nublo..46
Walk 6   Pico de las Nieves 52
Walk 7   Cruz Grande to Cruz de Tejeda 59
Walk 8   Roque Bentaiga 63
Walk 9   Cruz de Tejeda to Guía...68
Walk 10   Cruz de Tejeda to Artenara 73
Walk 11   Artenara to Tirma...76

Walk 12 Artenara to San Nicolás 81
Walk 13 San Nicolás to Tasártico 85
Walk 14 El Juncal to San Nicolás 90
Walk 15 Circuit of Inagua 95
Walk 16 San Nicolás and Viso 100
Walk 17 Las Niñas and Ojeda 104
Walk 18 El Juncal to Mogán 108
Walk 19 Cruz Grande to Mogán 112
Walk 20 Montaña Tauro 118

Fuerteventura 123

Walk 21 Punta de Jandía 126
Walk 22 Morro Jable and Cofete 129
Walk 23 Pico de la Zarza 133
Walk 24 Costa Calma and El Jable 135
Walk 25 Caleta de Fuste to Pozo Negro 140
Walk 26 Tiscamanita to Las Playitas 144
Walk 27 Tiscamanita to Valles de Ortega 148
Walk 28 Antigua and Betancuria 150
Walk 29 Morro de la Cruz to Ajuy 155
Walk 30 Dunas de Corralejo 159
Walk 31 Corralejo to El Cotillo 162
Walk 32 El Cotillo to La Oliva 166
Walk 33 Lajares to Corralejo 169
Walk 34 Isla de Lobos 172

Lanzarote 177

Walk 35 Puerto del Carmen to Playa Blanca 180
Walk 36 Playa Blanca and Los Ajaches 184
Walk 37 Femés Circuit 187
Walk 38 Femés to Yaiza 189
Walk 39 Playa Blanca to La Hoya 191
Walk 40 La Hoya to Yaiza 196
Walk 41 Ruta de Termesana 199
Walk 42 Volcanic Coast Walk 202
Walk 43 Caldera Blanca 205
Walk 44 Mancha Blanca to Monumento al Campesino 209

Walk 45   Jameos del Agua to Costa Teguise..214
Walk 46   Teguise to Haría 218
Walk 47   Máguez and Ye..222
Walk 48   Mirador del Río to Famara..225

Graciosa...229
Walk 49   Caleta de Sebo and the West..229
Walk 50   Caleta de Sebo and the North 231

Appendix 1: Topographical Glossary 234–235

INDEX OF MAPS

Gran Canaria general 31
Walks 1–4 33
Walks 6–10 51
Walks 11–15 77
Walks 16–20 99

Fuerteventura general map 123
Walks 21–23 125
Walk 24..136
Walk 25..141
Walks 26–27 143
Walks 28–29 151
Walks 30–31, 33–34 160
Walks 31–32 163

Lanzarote general map..177
Walks 35–39 179
Walks 40–43 195
Walk 44..210
Walk 45–46..213
Walks 47–50 221

Sunrise over the lagoon of La Charca de Maspalomas on Walk 1

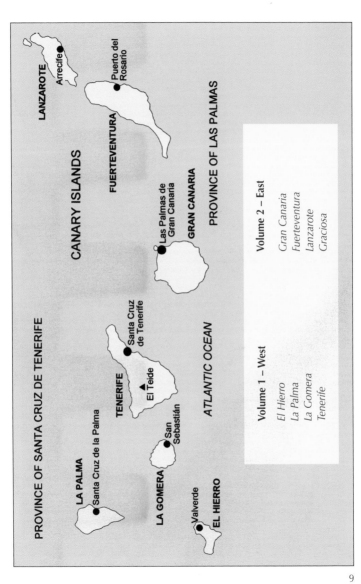

CANARY ISLANDS

PROVINCE OF SANTA CRUZ DE TENERIFE

LANZAROTE
Arrecife

FUERTEVENTURA
Puerto del Rosario

GRAN CANARIA
Las Palmas de Gran Canaria

PROVINCE OF LAS PALMAS

LA PALMA
Santa Cruz de la Palma

TENERIFE
Santa Cruz de Tenerife
▲ El Teide

LA GOMERA
San Sebastián

Valverde
EL HIERRO

ATLANTIC OCEAN

Volume 1 – West

El Hierro
La Palma
La Gomera
Tenerife

Volume 2 – East

Gran Canaria
Fuerteventura
Lanzarote
Graciosa

The Playa de Güigüí is accessible only after completing a mountain walk (Gran Canaria, Walk 13)

INTRODUCTION

The Canary Islands are a group of seven volcanic islands rising from the Atlantic Ocean off the coast of north Africa. They enjoy a sunny climate tempered by oceanic influences. Rainfall is rare and snowfall is confined to the highest peaks. Although the islands are often very rough and rocky, with impressive and often inaccessible cliffs, they are also crisscrossed with tracks and paths that offer a variety of interesting walking routes. Many areas are astoundingly beautiful and far removed from the major holiday resorts. There are mountain ridges and peaks to climb; deep and rocky *barrancos* to explore; extensive forests of pine and ancient 'laurisilva' woodlands; flowery hillsides, rugged cliff coastlines and cultivated terraces bearing all manner of fruit and vegetables. This guidebook includes a rich and varied selection of 50 walks on the islands of Gran Canaria, Fuerteventura and Lanzarote. A companion volume includes 50 more walks on the islands of Tenerife, La Gomera, La Palma and El Hierro.

LOCATION

The Canary Islands are more or less enclosed in a rectangular area from 13°30'W to 18°00'W and 27°30'N to 29°30'N. Interestingly, the small western island of El Hierro was long regarded as being at the very edge of the world; it was the original 0° meridian until supplanted by Greenwich! As a group, the islands stretch from east to west over a distance of 450km (280 miles). Although administered by Spain, the mother country is over 1100km (685 miles) away. The narrowest strait between the Canary Islands and north Africa is about 110km (70 miles) wide. There are seven main islands and a handful of much smaller ones. The total land area is nearly 7500km (2900 sq miles), but the islands occupy an area of the Atlantic Ocean nearly ten times that size. Apart from Morocco and the western Sahara, which are to the east, the nearest neighbours to the Canary Islands are Madeira, to the north, and the Azores, to the north-west.

GEOLOGY

The Canary Islands are essentially volcanic islands, and although much of the volcanic violence has long passed, there are still a handful of hot spots and there have been several recorded eruptions over the past 500 years. Magma from deep within the Earth spewed out onto the ocean floor over 100 million years ago. Gradually, enough material built up for land to rise above the water, so that the Canary Islands started appearing about 20 million years ago. The eastern islands of Lanzarote and

Handling a chunky volcanic 'bomb' while following the Ruta de Termesana

Fuerteventura surfaced first, followed by Gran Canaria, Tenerife, La Gomera and La Palma. El Hierro, in the far west, probably surfaced only in the last three million years.

The volcanic rocks seen today range from ancient strata formed millions of years ago to lava flows that spilled out as recently as the 1970s. There is every reason to believe that there will be further eruptions; most likely at the southern end of La Palma. Perhaps the most spectacular result of volcanic activity is the conical peak of El Teide (the highest mountain in all Spanish territory at 3718m), itself surrounded by jagged lava flows and the awesome crater-like rim of Las Cañadas. However, it is easy to lose count of the number of smaller volcanic cones that can be spotted in

their hundreds by a dedicated island-hopper. The deep-seated bedrock, volcanic dykes, later lava flows, cinder cones and almost everything else you see is essentially basaltic.

DISCOVERY AND HISTORY

Although the Spaniards are often credited with 'discovering' the Canary Islands, history has a lot more to say on the subject. The islands were convincingly described by Pliny the Elder in the first century AD, and it is thought he could have been drawing on information obtained by the Phoenicians or Carthaginians before the birth of Christ. Go back any earlier and the Canaries become lost in the mythology of Atlantis, but one thing is certain, the tribes known as the Guanches had already settled on the Canary Islands well before the birth of Christ, and Cro-Magnon Man was there as early as 3000BC. Where the Guanches came from, nobody can say for sure, though the simplest suggestion that they came from north Africa in fleets of canoes is probably the most plausible. Guanche civilisation has always been described as technologically primitive, even 'stone age', but was socially well ordered. The Guanches put up a fierce resistance when the Spaniards began their conquest of the islands from the 14th century, but one by one each island fell. Tenerife capitulated last of all, with the mighty volcano of El Teide grumbling throughout the conquest. Despite some of the Guanches entering into

Playing with fire at a volcanic hot spot in the Parque Nacional Timanfaya

treaties with the Spaniards and converting to Christianity, they ultimately lost their land and freedom, and often their lives.

The Canary Islands have been viewed as stepping stones to the Americas. They were visited by Christopher Columbus on his voyages of discovery from 1492. Their position has, however, as with most exposed island colonies, left the islands subject to pirate raids, as well as disputes with the Portuguese, attacks by British fleets and wavering economic fortunes.

There was constant rivalry between Tenerife and Gran Canaria, with the whole island group being governed from Las Palmas de Gran Canaria from 1808, but with Santa Cruz de Tenerife becoming the capital of the island group in 1822.

In 1927 the Canary Islands were divided into two provinces: Las Palmas and Santa Cruz de Tenerife. In the early part of the 20th century the military governor of the Canary Islands, General Franco, launched a coup from Tenerife. This led to the creation of the Spanish Republic, the onset of the infamous Spanish Civil War and a long dictatorship. The islands were free from the worst of the strife, but were also left as a kind of backwater. It was largely as a result of Franco's later policies that the Canary Islands were developed from the 1960s as a major tourist destination for sun-starved holidaymakers from northern Europe.

Since 1982 the islands have been an autonomous region and there have been a few calls for complete independence from Spain. The islanders think of themselves as 'Canarios' first and Spanish second, though they can also be fiercely loyal to their own particular islands, towns and villages. It is a pity that so many visiting tourists remain largely confined to the resorts and holiday complexes, and understand little about the history of the islands or the character of the people.

WEATHER

Most people have the impression that the Canary Islands bask in everlasting sunshine. While it is indeed true that they have an enviable number of sunshine hours and the lower parts of the islands are warm and balmy even in the winter, the mountains can be covered in clouds, wreathed in damp mists or even subject to occasional snowfall in winter. El Teide is high enough to catch snow every year and prominent enough to display it well. The high parts of La Palma and Gran Canaria may also see a little snow, but on the lower islands it is exceedingly rare and on the eastern islands it is unknown.

The prevailing trade winds blow from the north-west and tend to push a blanket of cloud against the higher western islands. The top of El Teide and the high parts of La Palma are often above the 'sea of clouds', while the uplands of El Hierro, La Gomera and Gran Canaria might be buried in

Remember that you are on islands off the coast of the Sahara Desert!

it. There can be a vast difference in the weather at sea level and on the high mountains, as well as between the damp northern slopes of the islands and the arid southern slopes. Shift the wind direction around and you can get anything from showers of rain – of tropical intensity at times – or hazy dust blowing in from the Sahara, though these conditions are short-lived.

In practical terms, most days will be hot and dry, though potentially uncomfortably humid. You should protect yourself against the sun and carry plenty of water to drink. If there is any likelihood of rain, then a lightweight waterproof will suffice, and if venturing onto the mountains in winter, be prepared for cold winds and even snow. Do not expose yourself to the sun for too long, and try and rest in the shade at intervals if it

feels uncomfortably hot. Keep reminding yourself that you are walking on a group of islands off the Sahara Desert!

LANDSCAPE

As a consequence of its volcanic origins, the Canarian landscape is often stark and severe. The islands are formed of layers of lava, some of which were weathered to a crumbly surface before being covered by more lava flows. The resulting beds of hard and soft layers weather most unevenly. Expect to find deep rocky valleys, or *barrancos*, and overhanging cliffs subject to rockfalls. Huge areas may be covered in soft pumice cinders that need to be emptied from your boots or shoes regularly. All the islands have rugged coastlines though sandy beaches are found on the eastern islands.

15

There are a few old buildings dating from the Conquest of the islands

Vegetation cover varies from absolutely nothing – or a mere dusting of lichens – through rubbery 'taibaba' scrub, to dense 'laurisilva' and vast areas covered in pines. Where the volcanic soil is supplied with enough water, a bewildering variety of crops can be grown. In some areas banana plantations or vineyards are extensive, while on some terraced slopes every kind of fruit and vegetable is grown. The landscape contains plenty of variety, but how much of it you experience depends on your choice of walks. While some walks include several types of landscape, others may confine you to a pine forest, picking a way across barren rocky slopes, or to a day hidden deep in the 'laurisilva'.

LANGUAGE

Spanish is spoken throughout the Canary Islands, and if you have any proficiency in that tongue you will realise that Canarios have their own accent and colloquialisms. One of the most peculiar features is the way the letter 's' often vanishes from the middle and ends of words to be replaced by a gentle 'h' sound. Sometimes the origins of certain placenames is rooted in the pre-Spanish Guanche language. In the big resorts there are plenty of people who speak good English and German, but don't expect many people in remote locations to speak anything other than Spanish. It is useful to learn enough key phrases to negotiate a bus journey or ask for basic directions, and you'll find most Canarios very patient and helpful if you make the effort to communicate in Spanish.

While using a map, it is useful to know what some of the placenames refer to, so consult the topographical glossary in Appendix 1 for some commonly used terms. Don't be surprised if other walkers or Canarios assume you are German and speak to you in German, as there are plenty of German walkers around. Don't be afraid to practise a few words of Spanish. No matter how bad you think you sound, be assured that the Canarios have heard plenty of really bad pronunciation and yours is unlikely to be the worst!

The 'sea of clouds' laps against the highest peaks on Gran Canaria

Canary pines have the ability to regenerate well after forest fires

Cardóncillo is an unusual plant that grows abundantly on one of the walks

ISLAND TREES AND FLOWERS

As each of the Canary Islands rose from the ocean, some attempt will have been made by terrestrial plants to gain a roothold. Maybe lichens and mosses managed to eke out an existence in tiny crevices, sometimes thriving, then being overwhelmed by lava flows. Later, a variety of plants, including flowers and trees, will have become established. The first seeds to reach these islands could have been deposited on the shore after floating on the ocean currents, or they could have been borne on the wind, or deposited in bird droppings.

The Canary Islands are remote from the African coast and have evolved a peculiar assemblage of plants that are not known elsewhere. While some plants may be related to others on nearby islands, or on the African or European mainland, others are unique to particular islands or even specific locations. Some striking and unusual plants are left over from the Miocene period, having become extinct elsewhere, such as the Dragon Trees. Some have adapted to particularly harsh conditions on the islands, such as the rubbery spurges, or *taibaba* and the thick candelabra spurges, or *cardón*. Canary pines flourish on many high mountainsides, defying the dryness of the ground and possessing an ability to regenerate even after severe forest fires. Some areas are densely covered in 'laurisilva' woodlands, containing various species of laurels and tree heather.

Uvilla is a small shrubby succulent plant that grows in coastal locations

Shrubby euphorbia grows in dry, rocky places all around the Canary Islands

These are the 'cloud forests' that sieve water droplets from the mist and keep the higher islands moist. Some of the lower arid slopes may be over-whelmed with Canarian palms, prickly pears and aloes. Flowers are abundant and form a specialist study. There are hundreds of flowers that are indigenous to the Canary Islands, and hundreds that are endemic. Even attempting to draw up a shortlist is futile, but anyone with a particular interest in flowers should obtain a good field guide to assist with identification of specimens. It is also a good idea to visit one or two botanic gardens, where most plants are name-tagged and information about them is close to hand. Keen botanists should visit the islands during May, when the flowers are at the blooming best. Good books inlcude: *Native Flora of the Canary Islands*, by Miguel Angel Cabrera Pérez, published by Everest; *Wild Flowers of the Canary Islands*, by David Bramwell and Zoë Bramwell, published by Editorial Rueda; and the more portable *Flora of the Canary Islands*, by David Bramwell, published by Editorial Rueda.

ISLAND BIRDS

The Canary Islands attract plenty of passage migrant birds, but there are very few full-time residents and a mere handful of endemic species. The laurel pigeon and rock pigeon naturally prefer woodland and cliffs respectively, and the former is becoming rather scarce. Although buzzards and kestrels can be spotted hunting in barren areas, the real hunter is the shrike, which feeds off an abundance of insects. Many of the birds you see around the Canary Islands are varieties of pipits, chaffinches, warblers and chiffchaffs. One of the smallest birds is the kinglet. There are canaries, though these have no connection with the name of the island group. Parakeets may add a flash of colour, and some birds have no doubt escaped from the aviaries that exist around the islands. The littoral zones are very limited, but the Canarian oystercatcher can eke out an existence there along with other waders and divers. It is best to take a boat trip to be able to spot such things as shearwaters or storm petrels, though gulls are common.

ISLAND ANIMALS

It is not known what animal life existed on the islands before the Guanches settled there. Perhaps the most notable creature to have survived, and then only in small numbers on El Hierro and La Gomera, is the giant lagarte lizard. There are a few species of smaller lizards that can be seen in most sunny places. Rabbits were introduced to the islands and are hunted by man and dog most weekends, and end up on many Canarian restaurant menus. Feral cats make ruthless predators against all small animals, surviving in the outdoors throughout the year.

The Guanches started grazing goats on the islands. The Canarios

The Guanches had a reverence for tall rocks, such as the Roque Nublo

have continued this tradition, making some areas look very close-cropped. There are some sheep and cattle, but these are only rarely seen; the usual array of farm and domestic animals are more common. Camels are frequently seen on the eastern islands as they were once important farm animals; they are now usually seen carrying tourists. Insect life is abundant in even the most desolate areas, such as Las Cañadas del Teide, where there are about 2000 species. In many places you see beehives, or signs warning of their existance. There are very few insects that bite or sting; it is safe to observe them, particularly the spectacular butterflies that sometimes flutter past.

You need to look to the sea to spot large wildlife. Whales and dolphins can be sometimes seen in great numbers. There are areas of the ocean near the islands that are sanctuaries for these animals. They can be visited on boat trips, which take you close enough to view them. Of course there are plenty of fish – more easily spotted on fish stalls than in the sea unless you include a diving trip in your exploration of the islands.

NATIONAL PARKS AND PROTECTED AREAS

Despite being of relatively small compass, the Canary Islands boast a higher concentration of protected landscapes than their mother Spain. The most important of these is the strictly controlled Parque Nacional, or National Park. Conservation often takes priority over recreation in these places, so walking opportunities may sometimes be quite limited, though the scenery is often of the highest order. In this guidebook there is one national park: the volcanic Timanfaya National Park, where visitors are generally forbidden to walk on the fragile landscapes.

Other commonly observed land designations include Parque Rural (Rural Park), Parque Natural (Natural Park), Paisaje Protegido (Protected Land), Reserva Natural Especial (Special Nature Reserve), Especio Natural Protegido (Protected Natural Space), Monumento Natural (Natural Monument), Reserva de Biosfera (Biosphere Reserve) and so on. The military maps show many of these areas, though without always assigning them specific boundaries. While rampant building schemes are observed around the coast it is heartening to find so much of the rest of the islands under some form of protection. This guidebook makes a point of exploring many of these protected areas as they are often of great interest and usually display spectacular scenery. Usually there are signs telling you when you are entering and leaving these areas.

GETTING TO THE CANARY ISLANDS

Flights
Most visitors to the Canary Islands arrive on charter flights from all over

Intricate terracing makes agriculture possible even on steep hillsides

Europe, but especially from northern Europe. Almost every travel agent in Europe offers competitive package tours to the Canaries, and most will be able to offer good flight-only deals on request. Charter flight destinations are usually to Tenerife, Gran Canaria and Lanzarote. Less often they are to Fuerteventura and rarely to La Palma. The small islands of La Gomera and El Hierro seem to be unknown to most travel agents! First-time visitors might be happy to fly to one of the popular islands, but those who want to visit the smaller and quieter islands will need to think about using onward flights or ferry services.

Inter-Island Flights

All seven of the Canary Islands have airports, and there are inter-island flights offering rapid (generally 15–30 minutes), though expensive, routes from one to another. Binter Canarias flies between the islands, with most flights operating out of Tenerife Norte or Gran Canaria. Flights from Tenerife serve all the other islands. Flights from Gran Canaria go to all islands except El Hierro.

Inter-Island Ferries

Ferries regularly ply between the islands. Heading east from Gran Canaria, slow ferries are operated by Naviera Armas and Trasmediterranea, serving Fuerteventura and Lanzarote. Trasmediterranea also operates fast ferries between the islands, though these are infrequent. Lineas Fred Olsen and Naviera Armas offer fast and regular links between Fuerteventura and Lanzarote, sailing between Corralejo and Playa Blanca.

23

Even the small islands of Lobos and Graciosa have daily ferry services. Walkers who want to cover more ground can also sail between Gran Canaria and Tenerife. Local travel agents can supply current schedules and can handle bookings. Ferry journeys can take as little as 30 minutes or as long as 10 hours, and are fairly cheap.

GETTING AROUND THE CANARY ISLANDS

Car Hire

Car hire is usually offered when a package holiday is booked, but it can be arranged on arrival or later. Cars can be hired from the airports and sometimes from the ferryports, or through travel agents and possibly through your hotel or local tour representative. However, because of the nature of the terrain, walks tend to be linear rather than circular, so a car is not always useful and is sometimes a liability. Many of the island roads are quite narrow and it can be alarming to meet large coaches on exposed bends. You need to balance the convenience of having a car with the inconvenience of having to retrieve it after a walk. There are plenty of useful bus services, and they are often a better way of exploring the islands.

Bus Services

Canarios don't speak about the 'bus' or even the 'autobus', but use the term 'guagua'. The bus station is the 'estacion de guaguas' and the bus stop is the 'parada de guagua'. Oddly enough, most bus stops carry only a single word – 'bus' – but you never hear a local person say it. When using timetables, please be aware that there can be differences in the level of service on weekdays, Saturdays and Sundays, as well as during festivals. Each island in this guidebook has companies providing bus services as follows.

Gran Canaria: Three bus companies on one island sounds as though things could be confusing. However, the Utinsa buses that cover the northern half of the island and the Salcai buses that cover the southern half of the island trade under the name Global. The other company operates the urban services around Las Palmas, which are only of use if you are staying in the city. A 'Tarjeta Insular' card can be purchased, which is accepted on all buses and saves having to fumble with change. Timetables used to be available in booklets containing all services, but now you're lucky if you can gather enough individual timetables to cover all the journeys you wish to make.

Fuerteventura: Tiadhe Bus services link the larger towns on the island, and there is even a night bus service linking Puerto del Rosario and Corralejo. Some smaller villages may have infrequent buses, or buses that run at inconvenient times. Walkers will sometimes find it easier to use an

The rough and rocky lava flows of the 1730s are pounded by an angry sea

infrequent service to reach the start of a walk, then finish in a place with more regular buses. A 'Tarjeta Dinero' can be used on the buses, instead of counting out change. Bus stations are almost unknown on the island, so get a single-sheet timetable from the Tourist Information Offices.

Lanzarote: Arrecife Bus services offer regular runs between all the resorts and main towns on the island, but some small villages have infrequent or inconveniently scheduled buses. A 'Tarjeta de Abono' can be used instead of counting out change. It offers ten journeys at a discount, yet seems to be rarely used, even by residents. Single-sheet timetables are available at Tourist Information Offices or at the bus station in Arrecife.

Tour Buses

Wherever you go in the Canary Islands, sooner or later you will find convoys of tour buses trundling along the roads. While these services are of limited use in reaching any destination, unless you consider abandoning them at some point, they can offer an easy insight into each island. A good all-round tour will include many of the scenic highlights, a couple of places offering food and drink, and maybe an on-board commentary. If the tour passes through the countryside or climbs into the mountains, then there is a chance to preview some of the walking areas or even

spot individual routes. After that, take to the public-service buses and then start walking!

Taxis

There may come a time when a walk is awkward to reach, or the bus service isn't particularly helpful, or a car is of little use – particularly on a linear walk. Most towns in the Canary Islands have taxi services, and there are more in the big towns and resorts than in small towns. Taxis tend to be expensive, but prices for long runs are always negotiable, and if the cost is shared between three or four people it can be quite reasonable. If you find a good driver, be sure to take his phone number and favour him with either a pick-up at the end of the day or another journey on another day. On some walks, it can be useful to take a couple of phone numbers for taxis so that you can bail out easily if you miss an infrequent bus or find yourself running late.

ACCOMMODATION

The bulk of visiting tourists reach the Canary Islands as part of an all-inclusive package deal. Accommodation is invariably provided in one of the major resorts, such as Maspalomas, Corralejo or Costa Teguise, in a major hotel or apartment complex. It is a system that works well enough for most holiday makers, but it may not be ideal for walkers – especially those who do not want to be tied to a specific location. Ask detailed questions about the precise location of your holiday accommodation before booking a package holiday, then check a detailed map to be sure that there is enough potential walking within easy reach, as well as good bus links.

Walkers who like to wander from place to place can easily book a flight and sort out accommodation 'on spec'. There are luxury Parador hotels, small hotels, apartments, *hostals* and *pensións* scattered throughout the Canary Islands. Admittedly, they can be very thinly scattered in some places. Tourist Information Offices can supply brochures or basic listings. Some farmhouses or country properties offer *casas rurales* (countryside apartments) for those who want to stay well away from the big resorts. Backpackers will have a hard time, as camping sites are very scarce. Wild camping is not permitted, and out-of-the-way mountain campgrounds require a special permit that has to be negotiated weeks in advance and may carry a limit of only a couple of nights in any one location. However, with such an equable climate there is nothing to stop you throwing down a sleeping bag in the wilderness for the night to bivvy out under the stars. It is hard to see how this could be policed!

Walkers who are not tied to packaged accommodation can travel from town to town, village to village, island to island, and generally please themselves where they go and what walking routes they wish to explore. Most walkers would be happy to stay in quiet mountain villages, far removed from the bustling resorts. Avoid the peak holiday seasons and there should be no problem finding a room for the night. At peak periods be sure to consult the available listings and phone at least a day or so ahead.

TOURIST INFORMATION

All the major towns on each of the Canary Islands have a Tourist Information Office. This may be ensconced in the *ayuntamiento* (town hall), or in a small building in a central part of town, or even just in a small room or street kiosk. Usually, but by no means always, English is spoken. Expect them to be able to offer some sort of accommodation listings, as well as information on transport and tours, and sundry visitor attractions. Do not expect to be able to get any detailed information about walking opportunities. Some of the offices may have a small stock of basic maps and guides, but it is often better to head for the biggest bookshop in town for a decent choice.

MAPS OF THE CANARY ISLANDS

Maps of a quality similar to Ordnance Survey (OS) Landranger or Explorer maps of Britain are not available on the Canary Islands. The Spanish equivalent of the Ordnance Survey is the Servicio Geográfico del Ejército. They produce both 1:50,000 and 1:25,000 Cartografía Militar, or military maps, of the islands. There are 29 maps in the 1:50,000 series covering the entire island group, and the relevant map(s) are identified at the beginning of each route description in this guide. Contouring on the military maps is good, and most landscape features are clear, but they tend to be out of date in terms of new roads and building developments. Many paths are shown rather vaguely or even erroneously. Some paths given great prominence on the maps may not exist on the ground. If you like OS-style maps, then these are the best that are available. Private mapping offers few alternatives, with scales and detail not really sufficient for walking. The Instituto Geográfico Nacional produces the 1:200,000 Mapa Provincial, which offers a complete overview of the islands. It gives a very honest impression of the relative size and position of each island, but leaves you feeling that you bought most of the Atlantic Ocean!

To obtain the military maps quoted in this guidebook you would be advised to order them well in advance from map suppliers such as Stanfords (12–14 Long Acre, London WC2E 9BR, tel. 0207 836 1321), The Map Shop (15 High Street, Upton-upon-Severn WR8 0HJ, tel. 01684 593146), or Cordee (3a De Montford Street, Leicester LE1 7HD, tel. 0116 254 3579). Simpler maps of the Canary Islands and free tourist maps can be obtained on reaching the islands. The sketch maps in this book are simply for reference. Transfer details to whatever maps are chosen, then use the route descriptions alongside while actually walking.

THE PLAN OF THIS GUIDE

This guidebook covers walks in the province of Las Palmas, which includes the main islands of Gran Canaria, Fuerteventura and Lanzarote, and the small island of Graciosa. The walking routes start with an exploration of Gran Canaria, on which twenty routes are offered, many of them linking with each other. Fuerteventura comes next, explored by a selection of fourteen walks in its southern, middle and northern reaches. Lanzarote divides conveniently into south and north, and fourteen walks, mostly interlinked, allow a thorough exploration. Graciosa is explored last, with two interlinked walks.

Cautious walkers should start with the shorter, easier walks. Read the route descriptions to decide if the walk is suitable, taking note of any difficulties mentioned. If using bus services, pace yourself carefully so that you are in time to catch the bus at the end of the walk. More adventurous walkers will find plenty of longer and tougher routes – some of them involving scrambling on exposed rocks, and some in mountainous country that needs care and respect. Walkers who really enjoy exploring the countryside on long walks will find that many of the routes in this guidebook can be linked end to end, forming long treks across or around the islands.

Each walk opens with a brief description, then has details relating to the length of the walk, start and finishing points, relevant maps, the nature of the terrain, bus services and refreshments. The route descriptions lead step by step along each of the routes, with the main features shown in **bold** in the text. Carry good maps, a compass and up-to-date bus timetables, then pace yourself to ensure that you reach the appropriate bus stop or pick-up point on time. The more remote or difficult the walk is, the more self-sufficient you need to be. Take enough food and water to drink, and try not to walk too long in open sun without taking a break in the shade. Use sunscreen, a sunhat and long-sleeved clothing to prevent sunburn. A torch could be useful if you go poking around in caves and tunnels.

Very few of the walks are circular, so using a car is a handicap when faced with so many linear walks. In deference to the steepness of the slopes, the heat and humidity, walks are sometimes downhill rather than uphill. However, there are many exceptions, and some walks are like roller-coasters with several ascents and descents.

EMERGENCY ASSISTANCE

Bear in mind that the Canary Islands have no organised mountain rescue service. If you need assistance, then it could be a combination of the ambulance, fire service and police involved in your rescue. All three services are contacted at the same emergency telephone number, which is 112.

Exploration of these islands can be continued with reference to the companion guidebook, *Walking in the Canary Islands, Volume 1: West*, which covers walks on Tenerife, La Gomera, La Palma and El Hierro.

The zigzag path climbing into the mountains from Cruz Grande (Gran Canaria, Walk 7)

GRAN CANARIA

Gran Canaria is the third largest of the Canary Islands, yet displays such a wealth of scenery and landforms that it has been called a 'continent in miniature'. Las Palmas is the only really big city in the whole of the Canary Islands, and there is an airport to the south of it. Ferries berth at Las Palmas, as well as at Agaete, where there are regular services to Tenerife. The island is essentially a vast dissected plateau, so the higher parts can be surprisingly gentle, while the valleys are deep and often exceptionally rocky. There are plenty of walking routes, but few are signposted or waymarked, and care is needed where steep and rocky slopes are encountered. Fortunately, many paths and tracks are very clear, including some well-paved paths that zigzag up and down cliff faces. The highest point on the island is Pico de las Nieves

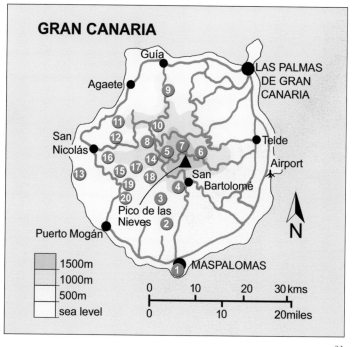

at 1949m (6394ft). It is the highest point in this guidebook, but is only half the height of El Teide on the neighbouring island of Tenerife. The uplands are often brushed by a sea of clouds, and the high pine forests are often damp and dripping. Contrast that with the lower slopes, which are arid and scrub covered, or even just bare rock and stones.

There are big holiday resorts in Gran Canaria, notably the twin resorts of Playa del Inglés and Maspalomas. But, there is also accommodation thinly spread around some of the smaller towns and villages, and even high in the mountains, so walkers can choose to stay in small, quiet places if they wish. Travelling around Gran Canaria takes time if you are using bus services, so it makes sense to choose two or three bases rather than trying to commute from a base that becomes inconvenient when some of the far-flung routes are being covered.

Walkers who travel around the island at an early opportunity will quickly realise that the northeast, east coast and much of the south hold little appeal, as they are covered with housing or offer poor scenery. The best routes are on the high ground in the centre of the island, and long walks radiate from there heading north, west and south. There are some rich and varied scenic landscapes in the west. Altogether there are twenty walks offered on Gran Canaria, and many of them are inter-linked so that it is easy to create longer multi-day treks that extend halfway across the island.

A view of the higher mountains from the easy forest track near Cruz Grande on Walk 4

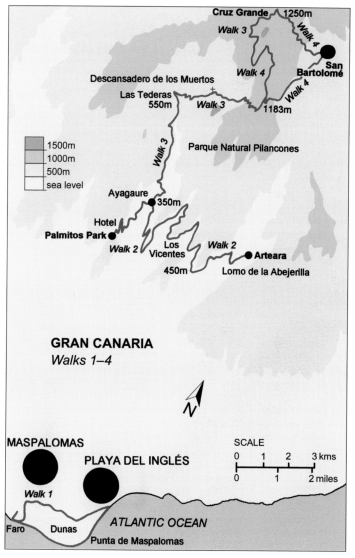

Cruz Grande 1250m

Walk 3

Walk 4

San Bartolomé

Walk 4

Descansadero de los Muertos

Las Tederas 550m

Walk 3

1183m

Walk 4

1500m
1000m
500m
sea level

Walk 3

Parque Natural Pilancones

Ayagaure 350m

Hotel

Palmitos Park

Walk 2

Los Vicentes

Walk 2

Arteara

450m

Lomo de la Abejerilla

GRAN CANARIA

Walks 1–4

N

MASPALOMAS

PLAYA DEL INGLÉS

SCALE

0 1 2 3 kms

0 1 2 miles

Walk 1

ATLANTIC OCEAN

Faro Dunas

Punta de Maspalomas

Sooner or later as you tour Gran Canaria, you will end up at the twin resorts of Maspalomas and Playa del Inglés. They are packed with amusements, food and drink, but more notably they abut the biggest heap of sand on the entire island – the Dunas de Maspalomas, covering over 400 hectares (1000 acres). In the evening, or more preferably early in the morning before anyone else gets there, it is well worth taking a stroll through the dunes. This can be as simple as walking along the beach, but it can be more interesting deep in the heart of the dunes, where there are three way-marked trails. The walk below wanders along one of the trails from Maspalomas to Playa del Inglés, then returns the along the beach (see the map on p. 33).

WALK 1
Dunas de Maspalomas

Distance:	10km (6 miles)
Start/Finish:	Faro de Maspalomas
Map:	1:50,000 Military Map Sheet 42-43
Terrain:	Low-level sand dunes and shore. The dunes are soft underfoot.

Leave the Estacion de Guaguas at Maspalomas and walk through the Plaza de Colon to reach the **Faro de Maspalomas**. This tall and slender lighthouse is a landmark even when you walk high in the mountains, so there is no chance of missing it at such close range! Turn left to pass the Hotel Faro Maspalomas, which overlooks a bouldery beach. A paved path, wooden walkway and another paved path lead to the Hotel Maspalomas Oasis. The paved path heads inland, passing a brackish lagoon called La Charca de Maspalomas and entering the Reserva Natural Especial Maspalomas. Pass apartments and palms by the reedy shore, then reach a road with a bus stop and taxi stand. A shelter full of information shows how the dunes looked in 1961, with the Faro being the only building of note. By 1987 there was already holiday development alongside the lagoon. By 1995, development was curtailed, following the demolition of the Hotel Dunas, which had been built in a sensitive area of the dunes. The area is important for its plants, fish, lizards and rabbits, though the water is a breeding ground for mosquitoes!

The paved path and road run inland alongside a broad, shallow *barranco* used by nesting birds. Cross the *barranco* before reaching a road bridge, using handy ramps on either side. A bird garden provides a cacophony of sound and flashes of colour, and camel tours are offered on the dunes. Climb onto a nearby high dune for a view of the full extent of the area, taking in the sea and scrub-covered dunes, backed by the resorts and distant mountains. Look down to spot a line of stout wooden posts ringed with blue paint. Go down to them, turn right and follow them to a junction with some red posts. Turn left to stay on the blue trail, which leads to the Centro de Visitantes at Playa del Inglés. The dunes are fairly stable at first, being covered by scrub whose roots hold everything in place. Later, the dunes are rather bare, and there may be puddles of water in some low parts, where rock and rubble may be exposed beneath the sand. Come up to a point where blue, red and yellow trails converge. There is an information centre just

Transport:
Plenty of Global Bus services link Maspalomas and Playa del Inglés, and there are also taxis.

Refreshments:
Plenty of places offer food and drink at Maspalomas and Playa del Inglés, and there are also beach bars along the shore.

After a windy night you can be the first to blaze a trail across the dunes

inland, devoted to the natural history of the dunes. The big building beyond is the Riu Palace Hotel, where the road is used by buses and taxis.

To stay on the dunes, take a concrete ledge running round the point, leading up to a broad promenade path. Either walk along the path for a firm footing or walk along softer ridges of sand. Whatever route you choose, the dunes are eventually pinched out by dozens of places offering food, drink and souvenirs. If you do this walk early in the morning, you may be too early for the full English and German breakfasts cooked up each morning!

You can bail out of the walk at this point, or simply turn on your heels and follow the beach back to Maspalomas. Bear in mind that topless sunbathing is common, and there is a long stretch of beach where nudity is the norm, although there is no compulsion to strip off if you don't want to. There are hundreds of sun-loungers at either end of the beach, as well as occasional beach bars offering cold drinks and ice creams. If it is too crowded, then you will find things a little quieter in the bare dunes just a step back from the sea. There is a broad sand bar between the sea and La Charca de Maspalomas, and the tall **Faro de Maspalomas** marks the end of the walk.

WALK 2
Arteara to Palmitos Park

Transport:
Global Bus 18 serves Arteara, linking with Maspalomas and Ayacata. Global Bus 70 links Palmitos Park with Maspalomas and Puerto Rico.

Refreshments:
Only the odd bar at Ayagaure and Palmitos Park.

Distance:	20km (12½ miles)
Start:	Arteara
Finish:	Palmitos Park
Map:	1:50,000 Military Map Sheet 42-43
Terrain:	Rough and rocky ridges and valleys, but the route is nearly always on easy and obvious dirt roads or tarmac roads.

Start at the roadside bus stop at **Arteara**, which is handy for Manolo's Camel Safari, but the narrow tarmac road leading into the village is a short distance back along the road in the direction of Maspalomas. This battered road leads through Arteara, passing a few buildings and fruit plots, surrounded by abundant palms. At the end of the road a narrow concrete path leads onto a heap of broken rock, then a narrow stony path continues to the left. Work a way round in a circuit across this chaotic heap of boulders, bearing in mind that the numerous cairns are all filled with cremated Guanche remains. The whole area is a vast burial ground. Climb up along a bouldery crest as if aiming for a water channel seen on the higher mountainside. There is a fence, but you should hit a dirt road just to the right of it. Turn left to follow this stony road, overlooking the bouldery burial ground from a fine stance. The general level of the dirt road is around 450m (1475ft).

Walk gently uphill and round a bend, then gently downhill, avoiding any tracks branching from the dirt road. Enjoy fine views along the length of the main valley while turning round the end of the **Lomo de la Abejerilla**. Rise gently across the slope to reach the head of the next valley, observing the rugged peaks above. Cross a bridge and start walking out of the valley, passing above a gap on a ridge, with a fine view of the Punta de la Cogalla beyond. Swing down into the next valley to face the higher peaks again, and cross another bridge at the head of the valley over the Barranco de los Vicentillos. Climb gently from the valley, passing a sign on the access track for **Los Vicentes**, then turn round the end of Alto de la Cogalla. Descend into the next rugged valley, and note that is it the longest of the series. Rather surprisingly, there are orange groves at its head. Follow the track down and cross the Barranco de los Vicentes, passing a little house. A long and gradual climb leads out of the valley, with increasingly rugged views of the surrounding mountains, ridges and valleys. There is a sudden sharp right turn as a gap is crossed on the ridge. The descent

This is a fairly simple walk along an obvious dirt road from Arteara to Ayagaure, followed by a winding tarmac road over to Palmitos Park (see map on p. 33). The scenery is often wonderfully rugged as the road runs in and out of deep valleys, crossing the rocky ridges that separate them. If it proves difficult, then it is probably because there is little shade on hot days, and the few vehicles that use the road kick up clouds of dust. There is no bus service from Ayagaure, but climbing over to the next valley provides access to buses from Palmitos Park, as well as a popular and interesting bird garden.

What looks like a chaotic heap of rubble at Arteara is a Guanche burial ground.

offers a view of **Ayagaure**, but the village takes time to reach as there are sweeping zigzags to negotiate on the mountainside. Cross a reservoir dam and head for a little plaza where the church and Bar Asociacion del Toscon are located. There is also a small shop. The altitude is 350m (1150ft).

Follow the tarmac road gently uphill from the shop, called the Tienda Ayagaure. The road rises, then falls as it swings round a little valley, then rises and falls again before leaving the village. Zigzags take it up past the two last houses, which are widely spaced and have big

gardens. Continue zigzagging up a steep and rugged slope to reach a gap at the top, at 492m (1614ft). Just before reaching a viewpoint on the left, cut off to the right and walk down a rough zigzag track. This leads to the Helga Masthoff Park and Sport Hotel, where there are tennis courts, palms and a surprising amount of greenery after the barren, rocky slopes encountered on most of this walk. Follow the access road down to the entrance to **Palmitos Park**. There are shady palms and pines, the sound of splashing water and exotic birds, as well as food and drink, if you have time to spare before catching a bus. You probably need at least two hours to make a decent tour around Palmitos Park to see the birds. If you finish too late for a bus, there are usually taxis waiting.

After crossing arid, rocky terrain, Palmitos Park is like an oasis of greenery

WALK 3
Cruz Grande to Palmitos Park

Cruz Grande is nothing more than a road bend on a gap, but it is the starting point for a number of fine mountain walks (see map p. 33). This particular route simply contours around the forested mountainsides for a while, then drops steep and rugged down into the valleys through the Parque Natural Pilancones. A towering pine tree flourishes in the middle of the walk, despite suffering several fires and grievous wounds. It even contains a visitor's book in one burnt-out hollow! The descent into the valley continues, and the route passes a reservoir on the way to Ayagaure. From there, a walk up a zigzag road leads over a high ridge to finish at the exotic bird gardens of Palmitos Park.

Distance:	21km (13 miles)
Start:	Cruz Grande
Finish:	Palmitos Park
Map:	1:50,000 Military Map Sheet 42-43
Terrain:	Forested mountainsides and valleys, mostly with clear paths, tracks and roads, but rugged in places.

Start at **Cruz Grande**, and note that the bus from San Bartolomé goes through the rocky gap before pulling in to drop off passengers. Walk back towards the gap, at 1250m (4100ft), and turn right down a clear track, then keep left, up past a little reservoir. Contour around a slope covered in pines, with a ground cover of guelder rose. Enjoy views of the mountains away to the right, and pass a sign announcing the Parque Natural Pilancones. There is a gradual ascent to a pronounced left bend. At this point, a path descends to the right, marked by parallel lines of stones, but save that for another day (see Walk 19). Stay on the broad track, descending very gently to a hairpin bend and a junction with another track. Down to the right is signposted for Los Bailaderos, Vivero and Pilancones. However, keep to the left, or straight on, and walk uphill a bit around a bend.

The track is a little narrower, but still clear to follow. It runs round a valley, down beneath a cliff that is undercut at one point, then rises gently with great views. Swing well to the left round a rocky point to enter the next valley. There is a slight ascent to turn round the head of the valley, then the track continues across the far side. (Alternatively, after turning round the rocky point, watch out for a narrow path marked by a couple of cairns, leading down to the right. This is rough and stony, but better later, crossing the valley and rising back to join the track on the far side.) You see a path rising to the left, and it is worth making a detour up to a gap for a view over to San Bartolomé. The track continues gently down to a gap, and there is a slight rise to a junction at 1183m (3881ft). Off to the left is a rocky path leading down to San Bartolomé (which can be explored with reference to Walk 4).

There is another Parque Natural Pilancones sign at the track junction. Keep right on the broad, clear track, first rising a little, then contouring across the rocky mountainside. Watch out for an obvious stone-paved path descending to the right. It becomes a narrower stony path, passing close to a giant pine tree. Guelder rose covers the ground. Zigzag downhill and don't be drawn along any other paths. A few stone steps lead onto and off the other side of a lower forest track. The way downhill is signposted as the Camino de Pilancones. The path is obvious and zigzags at first, then slices down across the valley side to reach another truly gigantic pine tree. This one is dripping with resin, so be careful if you

Transport:
Global Bus 18 serves Cruz Grande, linking with Maspalomas and Ayacata. Global Bus 70 links Palmitos Park with Maspalomas and Puerto Rico.

Refreshments:
Only the odd bar at Ayagaure and Palmitos Park.

Looking down the valleys from the pine covered slopes near Cruz Grande

sit in its shade, and sign the visitor's book if it is still lodged in the tree!

Huge boulders have fallen from the cliffs above the valley, and the path rises to a little cross with an inscription at **Descansadero de los Muertos**. It tells how the people of Ayagaure used to rest at that point while carrying their dead over the mountains for burial at Tunte, near San Bartolomé. The coffins were placed on a stone slab. There is also a note saying that the previous cross was replaced by the present one in 1994.

The path runs downhill, sometimes easily on a gravelly surface, and sometimes over rough and stony, or roughly boulder-paved, ground. It slices between cliff faces, and the pines begin to thin out as a wonderfully flowery scrub develops. Amaryllis blooms late in the year, and there are nut trees and prickly pears towards the bottom. Pass some little buildings and zigzag down onto a track. Turn left and quickly leave the track as marked by blobs of paint. Continue across the rocky slope, passing a few palms. Go down to cross the *barranco*, at 550m (1805ft), then go left up to a track, passing between two chained gateways.

Follow the track away from a *finca*, swinging round a side valley at another *finca*, then passing a third *finca*. Some land is under cultivation, with orange trees growing in places. There are no other habitations for a while, and the track stays well above the *barranco*, slicing across a slope sparsely covered in pines. Further along, houses will be seen down to the left and a big pine tree is seen near a junction of tracks. Keep straight on, crossing arid, scrubby slopes. There is a water pipe alongside the track, with a view down the valley to the reservoir, with the houses of **Ayagaure** above. Pass a white water-regulation building and follow the track downhill. Alternatively, walk straight down a path to cut out the first bend, then follow the winding track downhill and alongside the reservoir. Head for the little church and plaza, where you will find the Bar Asociacion del Toscon, with a little shop nearby called the Tienda Ayagaure. The altitude is 350m (1150ft).

Follow the tarmac road gently uphill from the shop. The road rises, then falls as it swings round a little valley, then rises and falls again before leaving the village. Zigzags take it up past the two last houses, which are widely spaced and have big gardens. Continue zigzagging up a steep and rugged slope to reach a gap at the top, at 492m (1614ft). Just before reaching a viewpoint on the left, cut off to the right and walk down a rough zigzag track. This leads to the Helga Masthoff Park and Sport Hotel, where there are tennis courts, palms and a surprising amount of greenery after the barren, rocky slopes encountered on most of this walk. Follow the access road down to the entrance to **Palmitos Park**. There are shady palms and pines, the sound of splashing water and exotic birds, as well as food and drink, if you have time to spare before catching a bus. You probably need at least two hours to make a decent tour around Palmitos Park to see the birds. If you finish too late for a bus, there are usually taxis waiting.

A series of small farmsteads, or 'fincas' are passed on the way to Ayagaure

San Bartolomé de Tirajana sits high in the mountains around 950m (3115ft). In the 16th century a simple *ermita* was built, and work on the current parish church began in 1680. Simple *hostal* accommodation is available in town, and there are a number of shops and bars, while above town is the splendid Hotel Restaurante Las Tirajanas, offering a grandstand view of the valley and mountains. Walkers who want a base away from the bustling resorts could stay up here. This route is a fine circular walk from town, climbing along a stone-paved path, contouring around forested mountainsides, then descending from the rocky slopes to the gentle, cultivated fields below (map p. 33).

WALK 4
San Bartolomé Circuit

Distance:	15km (9½ miles)
Start/Finish:	San Bartolomé
Map:	1:50,000 Military Map Sheet 42-43
Terrain:	Mostly steep forested mountain-sides, but paths and tracks are clear and well graded.

Leave the church and plaza in **San Bartolomé** and follow the main road as signposted for Tejeda. Turn left to follow a road up into the higher part of town, then turn right along the Calle Juglar Fabian Torres. When a telephone box is reached, turn right along a track signposted for the Camino Real to Cruz Grande. Continue straight along a path, climbing gently at first, then bending left and right to climb more steeply. The path becomes the stone-paved Camino a Santiago, rising by degrees across a forested slope with splendid views of the high mountains rising like a rampart across the valley. Simply follow the path uphill, climbing stone steps in places, then when a bend is reached on a prominent track continue gently uphill to reach a road and rocky gap at **Cruz Grande**, at 1250m (4100ft).

Walk through the gap and turn left along a clear track, then keep left up past a little reservoir. Contour around a slope covered in pines, with a ground cover of guelder rose. Enjoy views of the mountains away to the right, and pass a sign announcing the Parque Natural Pilancones. There is a gradual ascent to a pronounced left bend. At this point, a path descends to the right, marked by parallel lines of stones, but save that for another day (see Walk 19). Stay on the broad track, descending very gently to a hairpin bend and a junction with another track. Down to

Towards the end of the walk there is a bird's-eye view of San Bartolomé

the right is signposted for Los Bailaderos, Vivero and Pilancones. However, keep to the left, or straight on, and walk uphill a bit around a bend.

The track is a little narrower, but still clear to follow. It runs round a valley, down beneath a cliff that is under-cut at one point, then rises gently with great views. Swing well to the left round a rocky point to enter the next valley. There is a slight ascent to turn round the head of the valley, then the track continues across the far side. (Alternatively, after turning round the rocky point, watch out for a narrow path marked by a couple of cairns, leading down to the right. This is rough and

Transport:
Global Bus 18 serves San Bartolomé and Cruz Grande, linking with Maspalomas and Ayacata.

Refreshments:
Plenty of shops and bar restaurants in San Bartolomé.

45

stony, but it gets better later, crossing the valley and rising back to join the track on the far side.) You see a path rising to the left, and it is worth making a detour up to a gap for a view over to San Bartolomé. The track continues gently down to a gap, and there is a slight rise to a junction at 1183m (3881ft). The track continues to the right and can be explored with reference to Walk 3.

Follow the path to the left from the junction, which is rocky and becomes substantially buttressed as it swings left on the descent. It quickly drops below the level of the pines and zigzags down steep slopes of scrub. It runs along the base of a cliff and offers splendid views down into the valley. Turning a corner, there are a few more pines, and the track slices across steep and stony slopes. It descends into bushy scrub, while squealing and grunting gives due warning of a pig farm ahead. Follow the track down to a junction and turn left along the Camino del Pinar. This leads to the road, but remember to turn right at a junction along the way to reach it. The Hotel Restaurante Las Tirajanas can be reached by turning left, then right up the access road. There is a fine viewpoint at the road junction. To return to **San Bartolomé**, keep straight on along the road, then keep right and walk steeply downhill into town. The streets to follow are the Calle de el Roque, Calle San Juan, Calle de Corazon del Jesus and Calle Padre Claret.

Transport:
Global Bus 18 serves Ayacata from Maspalomas.

Refreshments:
There are a couple of bar restaurants at Ayacata, and there is often a snacks van parked on the road high above the village. There are a couple of bars off-route at La Culata.

WALK 5
Roque Nublo

Distance:	8km (5 miles)
Start/Finish:	Ayacata
Map:	1:50,000 Military Map Sheet 42-42
Terrain:	Mountainous, with rock outcrops and steep slopes of pine, but paths are generally clear throughout.

The little mountain village of **Ayacata** stands around 1300m (4265ft). It has a couple of bar restaurants, a little church, a plaza and a few houses tucked into a steep slope littered with enormous boulders. Follow the road uphill, signposted for Los Pechos and Cueva Grande. Take a rugged concrete road rising to the left to cut out a sweeping bend from the road. The concrete gives way to a rugged path before you reach the next road bend. A track rises from this bend, and the path is first to the left, then to the right as it rises. Pass a couple of buildings and follow the path as it weaves between enormous boulders on a slope of nut trees and scrub. When the path reaches the road at a higher level, turn left and pass a house called La Huerta Grande. Just round the corner, go up a flight of steps marked 'RN' between the houses on the other side of the road. Follow the path behind the houses up a scrubby slope to reach some pines and join the road again. Turn right, then look for the continuation of the path on the left. It zigzags uphill a bit, then runs roughly parallel to the road, finally reaching a parking space at the top of a gap at 1,578m (5,177ft), where there may be a snack van offering cold drinks, ice creams and local delicacies.

The Roque Nublo and other pinnacles are in view from the road gap, and a broad and clear path leads towards them. The path is often paved and well buttressed and can be busy. It climbs gently alongside a rocky ridge lined with a few pines. It climbs a bit more steeply up a slope of bare rock, with pinnacles often in view ahead. When the first big pinnacle becomes obscured by pines, watch out for a junction of paths and keep left, still climbing uphill. After much zigzagging the path reaches a rocky crest, then it becomes quite broad and gently sloping on the approach to the **Roque Nublo**. Approach with awe, and marvel at the monumental nature of the monolith. The main mass of rock is flanked by a smaller tower, and both can be approached closely. The Roque Nublo is undercut on all sides, and you could scramble all the way round its base if it weren't for one short stretch perched over a sheer drop!

The Guanche inhabitants of Gran Canaria had a reverence for huge landmark masses of rock. No rock comes close to the Roque Nuble for sheer dominance, rising as it does from a rocky plateau, towering above its surroundings, slightly overhanging on all sides. It is every inch a ritual object and has been designated a Natural Monument. The usual approach is from a road above Ayacata, but it can be climbed from the village, and for a little more effort a complete circuit can be made around the mountain (please refer to the map on p. 51). Even today, when you see people scurrying in droves towards this great monolith, you sense that none of its ritual power has diminished.

The rock casts a shadow across the landscape like a mighty sundial, and draws crowds of walkers to its feet. You may wonder if rock climbers ever make sport on it, climbing to the top at 1813m (5948ft). Look carefully and you will spot their bolts.

There is no way to leave the rock except by retracing steps back along the rocky crest. However, when the popular path heads down to the left, you can turn right down another path. It can still be a fairly busy route, leading down across a slope of pines and scrub, gradually descending and swinging low beneath the Roque Nublo. There is a path junction, where you could climb to the right to complete a fairly short circuit. However, head left down among the pines to pass an enormous boulder propped up by a huge boulder. The path steepens and becomes rough and stony, with a view back up to the crazy crest and all its peculiar pinnacles. Cross a *barranco* and walk among shady pines, looking back now only to see the Roque Nublo. The path runs level and easy among the pines, then descends rough and stony again. Go down into a *barranco* and cross over it, noticing odd outcrops of rock overlooking the village of La Culata deep in the valley. Continue down and across another slope to pass a ruin surrounded by nut trees. Cross another little *barranco* and pass a sign for the Monumento Natural Roque Nublo. Keep walking down alongside the pines, which are on a slope of monstrous boulders. Another path is marked to the right by arrows, and you can follow this, unless you want to go left down to La Culata for a break at a bar.

Detour to La Culata

The path runs downhill on a rocky, scrubby slope, where a rough and narrow path leads down past a few houses to land on a road-end. There is a path crossing the *barranco*, passing a little bridge and rising to a road. Turn left to walk down the road into La Culata. The Bar Restaurante Los Pasitos and Bar Roque Nublo offer refreshments. Beyond them is the plaza and church of Nuestra Señora de Fatima,

as well as a bus shelter, all around 1200m (3935ft). Buses are few and far between. When the village has been explored, retrace steps back up the valley to reach the path junction marked by wooden arrows.

The Roque Nublo and its smaller partner dwarf all those who approach them

Follow the path to the right to climb to the high road gap and return to Ayacata. The wooden arrows mark a zigzag path up into the pines. Sometimes the path is stone-paved and features steps, while at other times it is stony, or simply a groove full of pine needles. The zigzags lead up across a *barranco* and eventually to the top of the gap. The snacks van may still be parked at the roadside. All that remains is to retrace your earliest steps of the day back down to **Ayacata**. When the main road is reached down in the village, turn right to reach the Bar Casa Melo. The bus for San Bartolomé and Maspalomas stops here.

Looking down the steep and rocky valley to the village of Ayacata

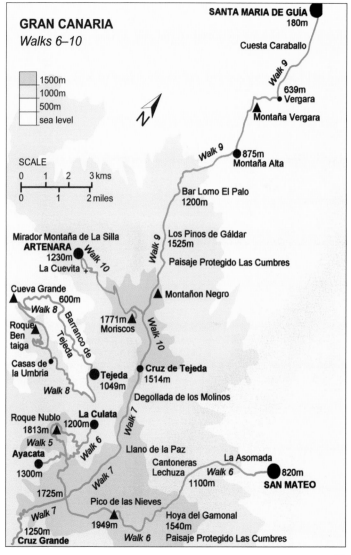

GRAN CANARIA
Walks 6–10

1500m
1000m
500m
sea level

SCALE

0   1   2   3 kms
0   1   2 miles

SANTA MARIA DE GUÍA
180m

Cuesta Caraballo

Walk 9

639m
● Vergara
▲ Montaña Vergara

Walk 9

● 875m
Montaña Alta

Bar Lomo El Palo
1200m

Mirador Montaña de La Silla
ARTENARA
1230m
La Cuevita +

Walk 10

Los Pinos de Gáldar
1525m

Paisaje Protegido Las Cumbres

▲ Montañon Negro

Cueva Grande
▲   600m
Walk 8

Barranco de Tejeda

Walk 10

1771m ▲
Moriscos

Roque
Ben
taiga ▲

Casas de
la Umbría

Walk 8

● Tejeda
1049m

● Cruz de Tejeda
1514m

Degollada de los Molinos

Roque Nublo
1813m ▲

La Culata
1200m ●

Walk 5
Ayacata ●
1300m

Walk 6

Walk 7

Llano de la Paz

Cantoneras
Lechuza
Walk 6
1100m

La Asomada

● 820m
SAN MATEO

Walk 7

1725m

Walk 7
1250m
Cruz Grande

Pico de las Nieves
▲
1949m   *Walk 6*

Hoya del Gamonal
1540m

Paisaje Protegido Las Cumbres

51

Motorists can drive
almost all the way
to the top of Pico de
las Nieves, the high-
est mountain on
Gran Canaria (and
in this book) at
1949m (6394ft). The
very highest point is
occupied by a mili-
tary installation, so
access is restricted
to a nearby view-
point. Walkers
would, of course, be
looking for a more
natural and chal-
lenging ascent. This
route starts from La
Culata and climbs
Roque Nublo first,
then aims to stay
high all the way to
Pico de las Nieves
(see the map on p.
51). An interesting
descent through a
valley and along a
gentle ridge leads
finally to San Mateo
to link with bus
services. Pick your
day for this walk, as
the mountains offer
wonderful views but
are often covered
in cloud.

WALK 6
Pico de las Nieves

Distance:	20km (12½ miles)
Start:	La Culata
Finish:	San Mateo
Map:	1:50,000 Military Map Sheet 42-42
Terrain:	Mountainous, often rocky under-foot, or with steep slopes of pines. Paths are mostly good, but there is one stretch requiring scrambling on steep rock. The latter parts are mostly cultivated, with tracks and roads being used.

The first bus from Las Palmas to Tejeda winds along the road to **La Culata**, around 1200m (3935ft), otherwise buses to this little mountain village are most infrequent. Have a look at the plaza and church of Nuestra Señora de Fatima, from where you can see the Roque Nublo high above. Walk along the road to pass the Bar Roque Nublo and Bar Restaurante Los Pasitos. Follow the road round a bend and watch for house number 52, where steps lead down to the right, indicated by a wooden arrow. A path leads across a *barranco*, passing a little bridge and climb-ing to a road-end. Continue uphill along a boulder-paved path marked by more wooden arrows, climbing above the last few houses. The higher parts of the valley are full of scrub and huge boulders. A path junction is reached before a slope of pines. You can take the path to the left to climb directly to a road on a gap, or take the path to the right and visit the Roque Nublo first. The latter is rec-ommended for the best mountain experience.

The path climbs alongside the pines, passes a sign for the Monumento Natural Roque Nublo, then crosses a little *barranco*. Climb steadily past a ruin surrounded by nut trees and follow the path up across another slope. A higher *barranco* is crossed and there are curious rock outcrops overlooking La Culata, now seen deep in the valley. The ascent is rough and stony, then levels out among the pines to progress more easily. The Roque Nublo can be seen above, and after another *barranco* is crossed, more of the crazy pinnacles arranged along the mountain crest come into view. The path steepens and becomes rough and stony, passing an enormous boulder propped up by a huge boulder. Keep right at a path junction, rising gradually and turning round the foot of the pine slopes supporting the Roque Nublo. At length, the path rises to the rocky crest of the mountain, where a left turn leads straight for the rock. Approach with awe, and marvel at the monumental nature of the monolith. The main mass of rock is flanked by a smaller tower, and both can be approached closely. The **Roque Nublo** is undercut on all sides, and you could scramble all the way round its base if it weren't for one short stretch perched over a sheer drop! The rock casts a shadow across the landscape like a mighty sundial, and draws crowds of walkers to its feet. You may wonder if rock climbers ever make sport on it, climbing to the top at 1813m (5948ft). Look carefully and you will spot their bolts.

There is no way to leave the rock except by retracing steps back along the rocky crest. This time, however, keep left to follow a popular path down to a road gap. The path zigzags downhill, and you should keep right at a junction among the pines. Big pinnacles of rock will be noticed above, before the path drops down a slope of bare rock. The rest of the path is easy, often paved and well buttressed as it leads to the road. There may be a snacks van parked here, offering cold drinks, ice cream and local delicacies. The height of the gap is 1578m (5177ft).

There is a choice to make before crossing the road. Staying high in the mountains requires a bit of scrambling on steep rock. If this doesn't appeal, then outflank the next stage by following the road; otherwise, cross the road and follow a vague, gritty, sparsely cairned path

Transport:
Global Bus 305 offers a limited service to La Culata from Las Palmas. Global Bus 303, 305 and 307 link San Mateo with Las Palmas. Global Bus 13 links San Mateo with Telde.

Refreshments:
There are a couple of bars at La Culata. Snack vans may be parked on the road beyond Roque Nublo and near the summit of Pico de las Nieves. There are plenty of shops, bars and restaurants in San Mateo.

Walkers follow an easy path away from the rocky pinnacles of Roque Nublo

up a slope of pines and scrub. Aim to reach the crest and drift gradually to the right to follow it. When a mass of rock appears ahead, drift to the left, then look carefully for the little cairns that show a steep and rocky scrambling route. You will need to use your hands, to be sure on your feet and to have a good head for heights. There is no need to go all the way to the summit, at 1763m (5784ft), which is easily passed to the right, but turn left afterwards and be sure to spot an old path, marked by a line of stones, passing an old fold. The path is discontinuous, but can be traced down to a gap. Climb from the gap and follow the easy crest, squeezing between scrub and pines. Trace a vague path until you interesect with a good path on a gentle forested gap at Degollada de los Hornos, around 1725m (5660ft).

Continue across the gap, following a narrow, sparsely cairned path through pines and scrub. The path rises across a couple of bare areas, and slices across the slope well to the left of the main mountain crest at Puntón de la Agujereada before zigzagging up to a stony gap. Stay fairly true to the crest for a while, though it is covered in pines and has only limited views.

Approaching the rocky top of a nameless mountain, there is a decision to be made. The path is marked by small cairns and shies off to the left before reaching the summit at 1926m (6319ft). However, there is a path to the right, and with a bit of hands-on scrambling you can climb to some of the rocky tors that make up the summit. The rock is a boulder agglomerate, full of comforting holds. Even if the summit isn't visited, views are very good, with El Teide on Tenerife often seen above the sea of clouds beyond the Roque Nublo.

Retrace steps back a little from the summit to continue along the other cairned path. Pick a way carefully down a rough and rocky ridge, using hands at times, steering a course between the cliffs and gullies to the right and the forested slopes to the left. When close to the end of the ridge, drop down into the forest and follow a vague path to a gap. Keep left of some huge boulders and rock outcrops, following the path through deep scrub and pines as it makes its way down to a lower gap. Squeeze up through scrub and pines along the narrow path until the ridge becomes more open and rocky. An easy ascent leads to a road-end viewpoint below the military installation on **Pico de las Nieves**. Clouds permitting, you can enjoy a view that can embrace Tenerife, La Gomera, El Hierro and Fuerteventura, but only in exceptionally clear conditions. Refreshments can be obtained if a snack van is parked here. There is no access to the summit of the mountain at 1949m (6394ft).

Follow the road down to a junction below the military installation. Just to the right is Pozo de la Nieve, where snow used to be stored in a deep covered pit. The pit was sunk in 1699 on the orders of the clergy at the cathedral in Las Palmas. Ice was periodically cut from here and carried at speed down to the city, where it was temporarily stored in a building called La Nevería behind the cathedral. The supply of ice was a commercial concern until the beginning of the 20th century.

Stay on the road, keeping high on the pine-covered crest. There are several ugly masts ahead around Roque Redondo, but you don't walk that far. Watch out for a square patch of tarmac to the left, formerly a helipad. Look down into a little valley that has steep gravelly sides, and pick a way down, along narrow paths, on the scrubby right-hand side. There are a few chestnut trees and other signs that the valley was once well cultivated, even at this height. A house is seen up to the left, but when a track is joined, follow it down to the road. Turn left up the road, then right along a track among the pines. Avoid turnings to the right until a cairn marks a path to the right. This is paved, leads back onto a track, then before the end of the track you follow another paved path. This drops down a slope thickly covered in bushes and can be a squeeze at times, but follow its winding course faithfully and it gets better at a lower level. It emerges into the open above a huddle of buildings at **Hoya del Gamonal**, at 1540m (5050ft).

Follow a track to the left of the buildings, then keep an eye open for a path descending to the left. This path merely slices a bend from the track, but the next path to the left is a winding forest path, leading down into the valley, becoming stone-paved along the way. The path crosses a streambed, then, by keeping right at junctions with other paths, you will be led down into a stand of pines, followed by eucalyptus, to land on a bend on a dirt road. Turn left to follow the road, which varies from hard-packed earth to concrete. It leads down through the lush, green, wooded valley, passing grassy terraces and offering fine views back up to the mountains. The road climbs gently, and to the right there is a view down to a little reservoir. Just up the road is a whitewashed concrete column, and at this point you exit to the right. Do not walk down to the dam, but walk straight across a grassy slope below some pines. When a track intersection is reached, go straight across and follow a broad track cut from a cinder slope. San Mateo can be seen way down the valley, tightly compacted, with its orange college building most prominent.

The track reaches the crest of a ridge, then continues onwards through a belt of pines to follow the crest. At a gap in the pines, look back to the head of the valley, and

Pico de las Nieves is the highest point on Gran Canaria at 1949m (6394ft)

down through the valley to see San Mateo, with the sprawling suburbs of Las Palmas beyond. Walk up over a cindery rise, then downhill roughly along the crest. The grass is close-cropped by sheep and goats, with pines to the right and chestnuts to the left, then later just the pines to the right. The more open parts look almost like gentle chalk downlands! A steep and gritty braided path leads down to a road, around 1100m (3610ft), where a sign points out that you are leaving the Paisage Protegido Las Cumbres.

Turn right down the road, passing a few houses and slopes of vines, as well as the waterworks at **Cantoneras Lechuza**. At a sharp left bend on a downhill stretch, head straight onwards, then uphill a short way, along a cinder track. Walk along this before heading down to a road. Turn right along the road to **La Asomada**, passing a telephone and a shop called Viveres Ojeda. Drop downhill with a view of San Mateo, then when a main road is reached, turn left and walk down a short, straight stretch of it. There is a bus shelter, where you can wait if a bus is due; otherwise continue down into the town as follows. Turn left down a steep concrete road, then carefully cross the main road at a bend. Walk down a track that becomes a concrete road called the Cuesta Majorero. Cross the main road again and follow another road straight towards town. The main road in **San Mateo** is reached at a point where there is a pizzeria on the corner. Turn right to pass shops, bars and restaurants before finding the bus station on the right, around 820m (2690ft). There are regular buses down to Las Palmas.

WALK 7
Cruz Grande to Cruz de Tejeda

Distance:	10km (6 miles)
Start:	Cruz Grande
Finish:	Cruz de Tejeda
Map:	1:50,000 Military Map Sheet 42-42
Terrain:	Steep, rocky and mountainous at first, but with good paths. The middle parts are forested and feature only gentle slopes. A series of paths along a ridge finally leads down to Cruz de Tejeda.

Start at **Cruz Grande**, and note that the bus from San Bartolomé goes through the rocky gap before pulling in to drop off passengers. Walk back through the gap, at 1250m (4100ft), and turn sharp left up a concrete access road. Pass a sign for the Monumento Natural Riscos de Tirajana and enjoy the initial view from some wooden crosses beside a house. Keep to the right of the house and follow a rocky path uphill overlooking San Bartolomé. The path levels out and there are views both sides of the narrow crest, then it climbs again. As it swings to the left it passes beneath a monstrous curved cliff-line, and does this with surprising ease, considering the nature of the terrain. Enjoy views down into the valleys, listening for the bongling bells of grazing goats, marvelling at the aloes that grow so abundantly on the rugged slope.

A broad, cobbled highway zigzags uphill among rocky buttresses, again with surprising ease. The route is well engineered and climbs onto bare rock slopes, where there is a little reservoir down to the left. Keep climbing, and the cobbles end suddenly on bare rock;

Undeterred by the massive mountain crest in the middle of Gran Canaria, early Spanish settlers applied themselves to the task of building roads across it, linking one village with another. Some spectacular stretches survive, not only displaying excellent engineering, but also offering fairly easy access to some remarkably rugged terrain. This route (see map on p. 51) follows a splendid old road above Cruz Grande, which climbs up a cliff and crosses barren rocky terrain. It continues through pine forests, but bear in mind that this part can resemble a huge campsite at weekends when local people take to the hills. A series of restored paths is linked along a ridge to head down to Cruz de Tejeda.

Transport:
Global Bus 18 passes Cruz Grande on its way from Maspalomas to Ayacata. On Sundays this bus runs as far as Cruz de Tejeda. Global Bus 305 serves Cruz de Tejeda from Las Palmas.

Refreshments:
There is a bar and restaurant at Cruz de Tejeda.

looking ahead you see only pines. Look carefully for a vague path worn on the ground, as well as the odd cairn and the scratches of walking poles, to continue gently uphill and into the pine forest. Although there are some short paved stretches, the route also crosses more bare rock and stony ground, heading back among the pines again. The path is broad and clear for a while, rising round a huge rocky valley, with views down to San Bartolomé and even distant Maspalomas. A cross stands above the path, on the left, then a broad and gentle gap called Degollada de los Hornos is crossed, around 1725m (5660ft). The path is clear and obvious as it runs down the forested slope to land on a road below.

Turn right to follow the road through the forest. While following the road round a bend, watch for two exits to the left, and take the second one. The ground is virtually level around Llano de la Paz and the track crosses it easily. Often it is fairly quiet up here, but some weekends can be very busy, when everyone in Las Palmas with a car and a tent drives up here and turns the place into an enormous campsite. Avoid a clear path heading off to the left, but a little later turn left along a path by a little streambed. There is a loop of track, and the path you follow crosses over the track twice. A junction of paved paths is reached near what appears to be a stone wayside cross near a road bend. The cross is actually a recent hunting monument.

Turn left at the path junction and walk gradually down across a steep slope overlooking La Culata. Although the path is broad and its paving has been restored, it is subject to occasional rockfalls. The path eventually drifts onto the ridge and winds downhill, often with a water pipe alongside. The ridge is covered in scrub and bushes, but stay on the most obvious trodden path and a few stone steps lead down to a road. Immediately turn left away from the road. Another stone-paved path runs down to La Culata, so leave it quickly by turning right and follow a narrow path between a house and the steep valley side. The ridge is covered in pines, and the path becomes vague and dusty, leading down to a gap at the Degollada de Becerra. There is access to a visitor centre, the Centro de Visitante del Parque Rural del Nublo, tucked into the mountainside at this point.

Just above the gap is a popular roadside view-point. Coaches often pull in for a photo stop, and there may be souvenirs and refreshments on sale. There is no need to follow the road. Simply look for the broad, stone-paved path running parallel to, but a good step above, the road. Keep to the right of a house on the way down to another gap and view-point at **Degollada de los Molinos**. Follow the road uphill to pass a slope of pines, then turn left up a stone-paved ramp to find

another path. A narrow cinder path leads up a scrubby slope to reach a bend on a broad cinder track. Follow the track uphill and pass between two fenced enclosures. A broad, level path follows a wall and fence, then narrows as it drops steeply downhill. Avoid turnings to left and right as the path picks its way through bushes. Fences define its final stages, and the path suddenly lands on a road bend at **Cruz de Tejeda** at 1514m (4967ft).

On the descent to Cruz Tejeda there are views of La Culata and Roque Nublo

Food and drink are immediately to hand at the Bar Restaurante Yolanda, which is part of the Hotel El Refugio. Across the road is the restored Parador. There are often stalls selling souvenirs and sometimes crowds of tourists. In the middle of it all is the 'Cruz' itself, which is an elaborately carved stone cross representing the Crucifixion. Buses from here run down to Las Palmas.

Unlikely as it may seem, the path from Cruz Grande climbs up this cliff!

WALK 8
Roque Bentaiga

Distance:	18km (11 miles)
Start/Finish:	Tejeda
Map:	1:50,000 Military Map Sheet 42-42
Terrain:	Rough and rocky for much of the time, with a steep descent into a *barranco*, an exposed and crumbling route through it, and a steep climb from it. The Cueva del Rey, if visited, needs special care. The latter parts of the walk are largely along roads.

The little plaza at **Tejeda** is crowded with the church of Nuestra Señora de Socorro, the town hall, library and local radio station. The altitude is 1049m (3442ft). Leave the plaza to walk down a steep and narrow road called the Calle de Doctor Heraclio Sánchez. This road winds downhill between tightly packed houses, often with cascades of flowers tumbling over their walls. Avoid all turnings and the road levels out, even climbing a little. A rocky knoll surmounted by a cross is seen ahead. At a bend in the road, take a path down to the right, turning left to pass above a little concrete water tank. The path descends, first passing terraces, then making a series of tight zigzags down through the scrub. The bed of the *barranco* is choked with cane, and just before reaching it note the concrete water channel cutting across the path, around 800m (2625ft).

Turn right to follow the channel. It is covered for a while, but when open, if there is any water in it, you will have to wade! Other parts of the channel are covered and there are some tight squeezes along its

The prominent Roque Bentaiga, rising to 1412m (4633ft), was one of the most revered sites for the Guanche inhabitants of Gran Canaria. Further down the rugged ridge they occupied a series of caves, of which the Cueva del Rey ('king's cave') is truly enormous. Starting from Tejeda (see map on p. 51), this walk goes deep into the Barranco de Tejeda and follows a crumbling old water channel. Be warned that one day this will crumble away completely, and the area is subject to rockfalls. Climbing from the *barranco* is tiring, but high above are the Cueva del Rey and Roque Bentaiga, waiting to be visited on the way back to Tejeda. This walk is for those with a sure foot and a head for heights, as it involves some short and exposed moves where hands might be required.

Transport:
Global Bus 305 runs from Las Palmas to Tejeda. On Sundays, Global Bus 18 runs from Maspalomas to Tejeda. The route can be finished early by arranging a pick-up with a taxi from Tejeda.

Refreshments:
Shops, bars and restaurants at Tejeda. There may be a cafeteria at the Roque Bentaiga visitor centre.

course. Cross an elevated stretch over another *barranco*, and if you don't like the feeling of height or exposure, then now is the time to turn round and climb back to Tejeda. Continue through thickets of cane and cross an aqueduct over the main *barranco*, turning a corner to reach some buildings. Follow a track here, omitting the next aqueduct. Do not climb up to the next little house, but follow the channel – although it is buried, it runs off to the left and can be traced by following a line of old pipeworks. The channel suddenly features a complex structure where the water falls suddenly, and you have to follow a little path down through the cane instead. The channel feeds a little watermill at this point, but it lies disused. Cross another aqueduct and continue easily along the channel, though it reaches a cliff with low headroom. Down in the *barranco* you can spot the first of a series of flood-control dams. There is another aqueduct, and if you look around the *barranco* you can spot all sorts of little houses and hideaways. An easy stretch is followed by another cliff walk. Looking back up the *barranco* reveals Tejeda; then, after turning a corner, the channel runs markedly downhill and the only settlement you see is Artenara high on the skyline.

The channel is often filled with stony detritus, and eventually another aqueduct crosses the *barranco*. The Roque Bentaiga stands high above, and you may wonder how you are going to reach it as the channel crosses another cliff. There is a view up a side *barranco* to Moriscos. Take great care where the channel is crumbling badly; when conditions dictate, shuffle along on your backside! One stretch of the channel is deeply buried, so continue along a good terrace and pause to enjoy the scenery. The channel crosses another cliff, then reaches an area around 600m (1970ft) that is always lush, green and damp, as there is a continual trickle of water.

Watch out for some tiny cultivation terraces and start climbing up a rough and stony path on the left. This zigzags close to a couple of storage huts, passes a

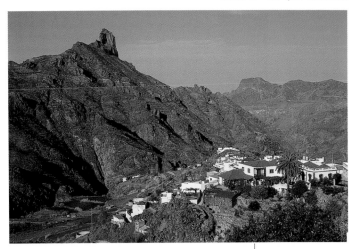

winch and passes below a house. Cross a rocky notch and be careful to locate the path beyond a landslip area. The path actually falls a little, passes a few little huts and runs into a *barranco*. Zigzag up the other side and don't follow dead ends to the huddle of houses at La Higuerilla. Instead, aim for a big derelict building that was formerly a school. Take a cue from the power line, which leads to the school building. A track makes a sweeping zigzag up to a road in the shadow of the Roque Bentaiga. Turn left up the road, which bends sharp right, then there is an access road for Cueva Grande, around 900m (2950ft).

Cueva Grande is a huddle of houses sitting on a windy, rocky gap. It proves to be an atmospheric place, but keeps its greatest secret well hidden. Zigzag up a steep concrete, stone-paved path to the left of the access road. Step carefully up onto a rockface to follow rock steps and narrow, exposed paths. Keep to the side of the cliff overlooking the Barranco de Tejeda. There are some small caves, and even a largish one with whitewash on the front, as well as a splendid view of the Roque Bentaiga. Climb more exposed, zigzag

From the start at Tejeda the Roque Bermeja is seen across the deep valley

65

The tiny settlement of Cueva Grande is perched on a remarkable rock ridge

steps to reach the unmistakeable Cueva del Rey. Be careful of the hollows cut in the floor, and notice how big the interior is when compared to the entrance. Carefully retrace steps to the road to continue.

Walk up the road from Cueva Grande, negotiating a zigzag stretch on the way. The road rises further, then a right turn is signposted for **Roque Bentaiga**. Simply follow this road, which works its way round the slope before zigzagging up to a car park at the Parque Arqueologico. The visitor centre incorporates the Cafeteria Bentayga, when open, so you might get a drink and snack here. A stone-paved path winds further uphill towards the rock, becoming quite rough and rocky. Follow the most obvious trodden path, which leads through a gap in a drystone wall on a rocky ridge. A stack of stone steps leads up to the 'Guanche Church', around 1300m (4265ft), where a curious cut has been made in the rock. Spend a while wondering how the Guanches revered this towering monolith, then walk back down the path to the visitor centre. Follow the road back down the zigzags and around the slope to return to the road junction below. Turn right to follow the road up to the **Casas de la Umbria**. A left turn here leads back to **Tejeda**. Although the town can be seen across the valley, the road is anything but direct and it takes a long time to cover. If you set out in the morning with the number of a taxi driver at Tejeda, then you can arrange a pick-up anywhere along the road, whether at Cueva Grande, the Parque Arqueologico or Casas de la Umbria.

Although it may look a long way on the map (see map on p. 51), the walk from Cruz de Tejeda to Guía, or Santa María de Guía, is easily accomplished. While the bus to Cruz de Tejeda gives a good leg-up into the mountains, there is still some climbing to do at the start. However, beyond Morsicos it is mostly downhill. The route includes interesting transitions from the mountains to the lowlands, as well as a glimpse into a deep volcanic crater, splendid areas of forest, and the odd bar and village along the way offering food and drink. There are bus services crossing the route if an early finish is required. Guía is a lovely old town and well worth wandering around at the end of the day. As buses run until quite late, there is no need to dash away after finishing the walk.

WALK 9
Cruz de Tejeda to Guía

Distance:	20km (12½ miles)
Start:	Cruz de Tejeda
Finish:	Santa María de Guía
Maps:	1:50,000 Military Map Sheets 42-42 and 41/42-41
Terrain:	Forested mountainsides gradually give way to cultivated lower slopes. Good paths, tracks and roads are used most of the way.

Cruz de Tejeda, at 1514m (4967ft), features the Hotel Restaurante El Refugio on one side of the road and a restored Parador on the other. The place is often busy with tourists and sometimes there are stalls selling souvenirs. Leave the hustle and bustle and walk along the road signposted for Pinos de Gáldar, and head round the back of the Parador. There is a turning area and car park, as well as a broad paved path climbing to the right of a transformer tower. That isn't your path, however; look for another path nearby, climbing alongside a stand of pines. The path leads up to a small hillside reservoir. Keep left to pass it, then climb up the rough and stony path among scrub and pines. The route is easier at a higher level, offering wonderful views across Tejeda, the Roque Nublo, Roque Bentaiga and Morsicos, and almost down to San Nicolás. The path exploits a soft layer, then goes down through bushes to a gap and road bend. A nearby viewpoint shelter takes in everything you've already seen, while across the gap is a glimpse of La Isleta beyond Las Palmas.

Steps and a paved path rise from a sign announcing the Paisaje Protegido Las Cumbres. The path is soon worn to bedrock, then it levels out in some bushes and enters a pine forest. Keep climbing to around 1700m (5575ft), then descend along a broad track. There is another fine view down a valley to Las Palmas and La Isleta. At a junction, turn right downhill on an even clearer track. Descend until there is a clear view of the bare slopes of **Montañon Negro** ahead, then watch out to the right for a direct descent to a road bend. There is a sign for the prominent Monumento Natural Montañon Negro. The mountain is bare to the right, covered in pines to the left, with a wall in-between and a tuft of scrub on top. Leave the road at the bend and follow a black cinder track straight down into the forest. When a quarried area is reached, keep to the left. The continuation of the track leads down among pines and chestnuts to land on another road bend. Turn left up this road, which carries the Las Palmas to Artenara bus service. Keep left at a junction as signposted for Artenara. Big eucalyptus trees stand in a line beside the road. On a high road bend is the **Mirador Los Pinos de Gáldar**, overlooking a deep volcanic crater. Views stretch round the coast almost from Agaete to Las Palmas and beyond. Refreshments may be on sale from a snacks van at the viewpoint, around 1525m (5000ft).

A path leads downhill from the Mirador, not along the crater rim but straight down from the little car park. The slope is forested and there are parallel drystone walls alongside the steep, loose cinder track. Further downhill the path levels out, then descends again and seems to terminate at a sign where you leave the Paisaje Protegido Las Cumbres. Step to the left to find a path continuing just alongside the crest. Later, a wall leads along the crest, and the side you walk along is quite bare, while the other side is covered in pines. The path drifts left from the wall, but if this isn't noticed turn left and let a fence lead you back onto the correct course. Both ways pass close to a little cross on the hillside. When the fence meets another wall on a gap, the path drifts to the right of the crest, then follows the crest, then drifts right to reach a road. There is another Paisage Protegido Las Cumbres sign here. Turn right to walk up the road, keeping straight on uphill as

Transport:
Global Bus 305 runs from Las Palmas to Cruz de Tejeda. Bus 220 passes the Mirador Los Pinos de Gáldar, linking with Artenara and Las Palmas. Bus 112 crosses the route at the Bar Lomo El Palo, running to Gáldar. Bus 107 links Montaña Alta with Gáldar. Bus 105 is the main service from Guía to Las Palmas.

Refreshments:
Bar and restaurant at Cruz de Tejeda. A possibility of a snack van at the Mirador Los Pinos de Gáldar. Bar Lomo El Palo at Risco Blanco. Shops bars and restaurants at Montaña Alta and Santa María de Guía.

The Monumento Natural Montañon Negro is passed to the left-hand side

signposted for Fontanales at a junction. The **Bar Lomo El Palo**, around 1200m (3935ft), is passed if refreshment is needed. Just round a bend is a bus stop and a limited service to Gáldar.

Turn left at a road junction next to a stand of pines and walk gently downhill. Turn left again at the third turning on the left, which is a clear track with a tall fence and a little hill to the right, and telegraph poles and a fertile valley to the left. At a bend, head down a broad, boulder-paved path, which is a bit brambly further downhill. Clip a concrete road bend and continue straight on along a good track lined with bushes, passing a few pines. The track is to the right of the crest, but later it shifts to the left, near a stand of eucalyptus. Follow the track down a slope of burnt trees and scrub, keeping straight on at a junction. When the track bends sharply left, continue straight on down a narrow trodden path between burnt tree trunks and scrub. When a remaining part of the forest is reached, fallen trees and scrub obstruct the path, but there is a road bend only a short way below. Head down to it and turn right, round a bend, to a road junction and bus stop.

Either turn left at the junction, as signposted for Guía and Gáldar, or use a forest path parallel to the road. The gentle ridge path has pines along it, but also resprouting eucalyptus stumps. Continue along the road called the Calle Piedra de Molino, walking gently downhill, passing houses and bus stops. There are a number of places offering food and drink as the road drops more steeply into the little village of **Montaña Alta**. There is a church on the little Plaza San Jose de la Montaña, around 875m (2870ft).

Turn left along a narrow road beside the church to leave the village. This is the Calle Fuente Bermeja, and it runs gently downhill, overlooking terraces and houses in the valley. Caves have been cut from the rockface on the right, then there are a few more houses. When the road suddenly bends right to drop to a main road, turn left down a narrow path left along a little ridge. Turn right at the bottom to pass a wayside shrine and bus shelter, then turn left along the main road. Take a minor road down to the left, slicing across the slopes of **Montaña Vergara** and looking across a cultivated landscape. There is a sharp turn to the right, and you walk almost to the house at the end of the road. Just before it, turn left along a narrow path. This rises gently and passes a water tank and a prominent terrace, then continues as a clear track. When a concrete road is joined, turn right and follow it to a junction with a narrow tarmac road. Turn right again and follow the road, climbing almost to join the main road again at **Vergara**, at 639m (2096ft).

Just before reaching the main road, turn left along a patchy concrete road. Follow this until a clear track descends from it. The road becomes concrete again, passing a few houses to return to the main road. Walk straight along the road to reach a junction. Although Guía is signposted straight on, you should fork left as signposted for **Cuesta Caraballo**. This road stays high and enjoys reasonable views, passing houses, cultivated areas and gardens, then it suddenly steepens and is covered in concrete. It leads down to the Hospital de San

Towards the end of the walk, Guía is seen below, with Gáldar beyond

Roque, and the Avenida de España leads further downhill from there. Walk through the new Plaza San Roque, then straight down past the church and the lovely old Plaza San Roque. There is a bar here; otherwise walk down the Calle Pérez Galdós and pass San Antonio. A quick left and right turn at the bottom leads to a big church and the Plaza Grande in **Guía**, around 180m (590ft). Enjoy the old part of town, then keep heading down into the new part of town to find the bus stops.

WALK 10
Cruz de Tejeda to Artenara

Distance:	10km (6 miles)
Start:	Cruz de Tejeda
Finish:	Artenara
Map:	1:50,000 Military Map Sheet 42-42
Terrain:	Fairly gentle forested uplands and more open lower slopes. The route includes good paths and tracks.

Cruz de Tejeda, at 1,514m (4,967ft), features the Hotel Restaurante El Refugio on one side of the road and a restored Parador on the other. The place is often busy with tourists and sometimes there are stalls selling souvenirs. Leave the hustle and bustle and walk along the road signposted for Pinos de Gáldar, and head round the back of the Parador. There is a turning area and car park, as well as a broad paved path climbing to the right of a transformer tower. That isn't your path, however; look for another path nearby, climbing alongside a stand of pines. The path leads up to a small hillside reservoir. Keep left to pass it, then climb up the rough and stony path among scrub and pines. The route is easier at a higher level, offering wonderful views across Tejeda, the Roque Nublo, Roque Bentaiga and Moriscos, and almost down to San Nicolás. The path exploits a soft layer, then goes down through bushes to a gap and road bend. A nearby viewpoint shelter takes in everything you've already seen, while across the gap is a glimpse of La Isleta beyond Las Palmas.

Steps and a paved path rise from a sign announcing the Paisaje Protegido Las Cumbres. The path is soon worn to bedrock, then it levels out in some bushes and enters a pine forest. Keep climbing, then descend along

This short walk (see map on p. 51) leaves plenty of time to take things easy and enjoy the ascent of the forested mountain of Moriscos and the wonderful views that feature on a clear day. Take the time to wander round the old mountain village of Artenara. In particular, take the splendid mountainside path to the Ermita de La Virgen de La Cuevita. This interesting little chapel, including the altar and other features, has been carved from solid rock. The area outside is often a riot of colourful flowers. On the other side of Artenara is a hill crowned with a statue of Christ, while a tunnel through the hill leads to a restaurant perched on a balcony, where you can dine under an overhang with a magnificent view across the valley to the mountains.

Transport:
Global Bus 305 runs from Las Palmas to Cruz de Tejeda.
Global Bus 220 links Artenara with Las Palmas.

Refreshments:
Bar and restaurant at Cruz de Tejeda. A number of shops, bars and restaurants at Artenara.

There are some fine views on the descent from the forested Moriscos

a broad track. There is another fine view down a valley to Las Palmas and La Isleta. At a junction with a clearer track, turn left uphill. The track rises, with dense pines up to the left and a mixture of pines and chestnuts down to the right. Avoid a right turn, and walk straight onwards to reach a junction of tracks high on the shoulder of Moriscos. There is an old stone cross at this point, around 1700m (5575ft). To include the summit of **Moriscos**, turn left and simply follow the track uphill.

The view is partly obscured by pines and communication equipment on the summit, though there is a fire tower offering a bit more height. The trig point stands at 1771m (5810ft). Back at the track junction, however, if you don't want to climb Moriscos, then a right turn leads quickly to a fine viewpoint. To continue with the walk, simply walk straight through the junction, and the track winds downhill on a slope of pines. At one bend, be sure to take in the view from a gap on the left, which includes the mighty Roque Bentaiga and the high Cumbre. There are some huge boulders on the left, then the track rises gently. Descend further, with views to the right taking in terraces and buildings. Big bends lead round and down

into another forested valley. Further down the white dusty track is a junction on a bend. Head left, which is in effect straight on, down a narrower and stonier track, with a drystone wall to the right. Pines stand to the right and scrubby slopes to the left, with a couple of cultivated plots at the bottom, as well as old terraces.

At another junction, keep walking straight ahead down the track. Watch for a stony path heading down to the right, which cuts a bend from the track. Watch for another path, initially stone-paved, also heading down to the right. It winds down in eroded zigzags, and by keeping left you reach a rocky notch with a narrow road running through it. Take a peek on the far side of this notch for the splendid views, then come back through and turn left. Immediately, keep to the right of a stand of pines, and keep on the right-hand side of the high crest to reach a fork in the track. Keep right again, then swing left round the hillside for a sudden view of Artenara huddled on a gap below, at 1230m (4035ft). On reaching a tarmac road, simply walk downhill, but watch for a signpost pointing left for **La Virgen de La Cuevita**. Follow the road to its end and continue along a broad paved path,

A tall statue of Christ embraces the little mountain village of Artenara

rich with flowers, to reach the cave-chapel. Spend a moment in meditation, then walk back along the path and road to **Artenara**.

The village is quite compact and has shops, bars and restaurants. The church of San Matias was founded on the site of a 17th-century *ermita*. The valley below the centre of Artenara is a tree-shaded recreation area called the Parque Manuel Diaz Cruz. Follow a road up towards the hill bearing a statue of Christ to find a short path leading to the summit. The statue was raised in 1996 and there are splendid views from it. On the way there you will notice a tunnel through the hill that leads to the interesting Mirador Montaña de La Silla and an unusual restaurant tucked into an ivy-clad overhang.

WALK 11
Artenara to Tirma

Transport:
Global Bus 220 serves Artenara from Las Palmas. Global Bus 101 links the Morro de la Campana, near Tirma, with San Nicolás and Las Palmas.

Refreshments:
Shops, bars and restaurants at Artenara only.

Distance:	21km (13 miles)
Start:	Artenara
Finish:	Morro de la Campana, near Tirma
Maps:	1:50,000 Military Map Sheets 41-42 and 42-42
Terrain:	Mostly forested mountainsides, with fairly gentle gradients using good paths, tracks and roads.

Leave **Artenara**, at an altitude of 1230m (4035ft), by following a road downhill to a roundabout. Go straight through to follow a road steeply uphill, signposted for the *cementerio* (cemetery). The road is quite broad at the top, and just as the cemetery and a helipad come into view, turn left up a road that quickly becomes a dirt track. Follow the track to a junction, where a narrow path heads off to the left and the track continues rising to the right. Walk along the track, passing pines and eucalyptus to reach a scrubby slope where a red

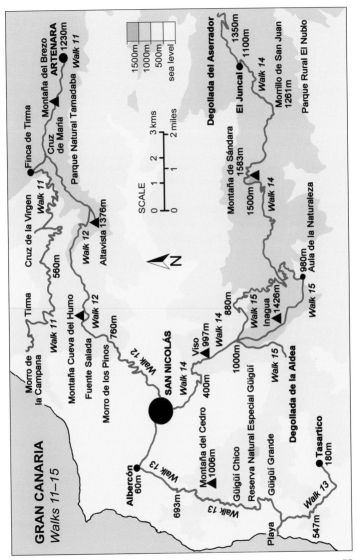

GRAN CANARIA
Walks 11–15

ARTENARA 1230m
Montaña del Brezo
Finca de Tirma
Cruz de María
Parque Natural Tamadaba *Walk 11*
Cruz de la Virgen *Walk 11*
Tirma
Morro de la Campana
Walk 11
560m
Walk 12
Altavista 1376m
Montaña Cueva del Humo *Walk 12*
Fuente Salada
760m
Morro de los Pinos
Walk 12
Viso 997m *Walk 14*
SAN NICOLÁS *Walk 14*
400m
880m
1000m
Inagua 1426m *Walk 15*
Montaña del Cedro 1006m
Güigüí Chico
Reserva Natural Especial Güigüí
Güigüí Grande *Walk 15*
Degollada de la Aldea
Albercón 60m
Walk 13
693m
Walk 13
Playa
547m
Walk 13
Tasartico 180m

Degollada del Aserrador 1350m
El Juncal 1100m *Walk 14*
Morrillo de San Juan 1261m
Parque Rural El Nublo
Montaña de Sándara 1583m
1500m *Walk 14*
980m Aula de la Naturaleza *Walk 15*

1500m
1000m
500m
sea level

SCALE
0   1   2   3 kms
0   1   2 miles

N

77

There are two ways to cover this route (see map on p. 77). The first half of the route is a simple walk over the slopes of Montaña del Brezo. After that, a return could be made by following the road back to Artenara. You could take a taxi from Artenara to the Finca de Tirma, then simply follow the broad and obvious forest road until the main coast road is reached at a convenient bus shelter. The full route from Artenara to Tirma and the coast road isn't too demanding for a walker, but you need to pace yourself and be sure of the bus timetables to meet a bus on the lonely coast road at the end.

and white mast is passed. The summit of **Montaña del Brezo** is rocky, so the path slices off to the right, crossing the rocky slopes with ease around 1300m (4265ft). It descends more steeply, with a few steps along the way, among dense pines. There are more open views later and there is occasionally a water pipe alongside. Zigzag down a stony path to land on the road beside a sign for Montaña del Brezo. Turn left and walk straight through a crossroads as signposted for Pinar de Tamadaba.

Walk gently down the bendy road, but just before reaching a sign for El Pinar, around 1100m (3610ft), step to the left through the roadside barrier, where a short stretch of paved path leads uphill. The path is a bit rocky at first, then it becomes well graded, rising up a slope of pines with a rampant ground cover of guelder rose. The path is never far from the road and eventually joins it again where a sign announces that you are leaving the Parque Rural El Nublo. Turn left up the road but exit at the next bend, where there is a viewpoint looking towards the high mountains, including Pico de las Nieves, Roque Nublo and Roque Bentaiga. A path climbing uphill is signposted as the Camino Cruz de Maria la Aldea. Walk up this path, and note how ropy strands of lichen grow on all the tree branches. When a prominent junction of paths is reached, around 1240m (4070ft), turn right downhill. The other path leads to Altavista and forms part of Walk 12. Follow this path across a forested slope roughly parallel to the road. It eventually drops to the road near the **Finca de Tirma** at 1184m (3885ft).

Step past a gate pillar at this lovely little forestry house, then swing left to follow the forest road downhill. The slopes are covered in pine and the dirt road is very bendy indeed, so you will find yourself looking at everything along the way from several directions! The track has been cut from rock in places and there are always whitewashed stones arranged along the outside edge. Views stretch up to the mountains and down to the sea, and often include many of the bends ahead to be negotiated. As the track works its way round the head of the Barranco del Vaquero it passes a dry waterfall, then turns a prominent corner and drifts gently down around another valley. There are sweeping zigzags down to a junction at El Vaquero. A right turn leads to a small reservoir and house, which are private, so keep left and rise gently away. Turn round another valley, then follow a spur track out onto a promontory at the Mirador **Cruz de la Virgen**, around 880m (2885ft). Views inland are limited by the height of Altavista, but looking down the valleys to the sea is dramatic.

Continue along the main track, which runs gently downhill, then embarks on a long descent made up of interminable bends and zigzags. Looking downhill the sheer number of zigzags seems almost comical, and following them ensures that you will appreciate the Barranco Hoya del Laurel from every possible vantage point. The *barranco* is finally crossed in a deep, steep-sided rocky valley. Water is drawn off just above the bridge. The pine cover on the lower slopes is sparse and the track runs gently downhill, winding in and out

There are fine views on the final descent to the main road beyond Tirma

of little valleys on the mountainside. There is another zigzag, then the track approaches the Casa de la Marquesa, at 560m (1835ft). To the right is a track signposted as the Camino Real Tirma–El Risco, offering a rapid descent to the village of El Risco and the main road if one is needed. The track you followed here is signposted back for Tamadaba, which leaves a left turn signposted for Anden Verde.

Follow the bendy track gently uphill. There is often a water pipe alongside, while the slopes covered in cistus are slowly being reforested. Keep rising gradually around barren valleys, noting the unusual pastel colours in the bedrock. A left turn is signposted for Cueva Nueva Tafaraca, but stay on the main track and work your way round one last big barren valley to reach a house at Tirma. There are huge prickly pears here, as well as a wonderful mixture of trees, shrubs and flowers. Pass a barrier and note a rocky knoll covered in candelabra spurge, at 696m (2283ft). The track bends sharp left and heads downhill with a view of rocky ridges falling steeply towards the sea. Puerto de las Nieves can be seen along the coast. Look out for a little shrine tucked into the mountainside on the left. The track finally zigzags down to a sign for Finca de Tirma. There is a bus shelter beside the road at 550m (1805ft) at Morro de la Campana. Be sure of the bus timetables and make sure that the bus driver can see you. This is a remote stretch of road to reach if you miss the bus and have no other transport available.

WALK 12
Artenara to San Nicolás

Distance:	23km (14¼ miles)
Start:	Artenara
Finish:	San Nicolás
Maps:	1:50,000 Military Map Sheets 41-42 and 42-42
Terrain:	Forested mountainsides and ridges give way to steep and rocky slopes and a long, broad, knobbly ridge. There is a steep descent at the end of the day. Good paths and tracks are used most of the way.

Leave **Artenara**, at an altitude of 1230m (4035ft), by following a road downhill to a roundabout. Go straight through to follow a road steeply uphill, signposted for the *cementerio* (cemetery). The road is quite broad at the top, and just as the cemetery and a helipad come into view turn left up a road that quickly becomes a dirt track. Follow the track to a junction, where a narrow path heads off to the left and the track continues rising to the right. Walk along the track, passing pines and eucalyptus to reach a scrubby slope, where a red and white mast is passed. The summit of **Montaña del Brezo** is rocky, so the path slices off to the right, crossing the rocky slopes with ease around 1300m (4265ft). It descends more steeply, with a few steps along the way, among dense pines. There are more open views later and there is occasionally a water pipe alongside. Zigzag down a stony path to land on the road beside a sign for Montaña del Brezo. Turn left and walk straight through a crossroads as signposted for Pinar de Tamadaba.

Walk gently down the bendy road, but just before reaching a sign for El Pinar, around 1100m (3610ft), step

This is a long walk that leads into wonderfully remote and wild countryside (see map p. 77). You could shorten it by taking a taxi from Artenara, along the Tamadaba road, to the beginning of the path climbing Altavista. The ascent of Altavista is highly recommended as it is a notable viewpoint, but you could omit the summit and simply continue along to San Nicolás. The rollercoaster path wanders along a knobbly ridge, staying high until its final descent to San Nicolás. If you are staying in San Nicolás then you can take your time getting there, but if you have a bus to catch, take careful note of the timetables. The journey back to Las Palmas is one of the longest bus runs on Gran Canaria.

Transport:
Global Bus 220
serves Artenara. Taxis
are available in
Artenara. Global Bus
38 and 101 run
south and north
respectively to link
San Nicolás with Las
Palmas.

Refreshments:
Shops, bars and
restaurants at
Artenara and San
Nicolás.

to the left through the roadside barrier, where a short stretch of paved path leads uphill. The path is a bit rocky at first, then it becomes well graded, rising up a slope of pines with a rampant ground cover of guelder rose. The path is never far from the road, and eventually joins it again where a sign announces that you are leaving the Parque Rural El Nublo. Turn left up the road but exit at the next bend, where there is a viewpoint looking towards the high mountains, including Pico de las Nieves, Roque Nublo and Roque Bentaiga. A path climbing uphill is signposted as the Camino Cruz de Maria la Aldea. Walk up this path, and note how ropy strands of lichen grow on all the tree branches. When a prominent junction of paths is reached, keep left uphill. The other path goes down to the Finca de Tirma and is part of Walk 11. Keep climbing, and the path passes a wayside cross, the **Cruz de Maria**, around 1250m (4100ft).

A major part of the ascent is already completed, and, if anything, the path runs level or even descends slightly and runs to one side or the other of the pine ridge. One moment there are views inland to the high Cumbre, while the next moment there is a view down to the sea at El Risco. There is a gentle ascent and a bend, followed by a descent to a gap, where things are a bit rockier. Climb again to the right of a forested peak, often on steep slopes, but with no sense of exposure. Reach another gap and climb uphill again, with views of the Cumbre beyond Artenara and Acusa. Turn round a corner and zigzag down a steep and rocky slope to reach a rocky gap. The ridge is almost a knife-edge at this point, and you can pick a way across if you wish, but the path shies downhill to outflank it. Beyond the gap there are three paths. The one to the extreme left is not used. The middle one leads only to the summit of Altavista, while the one on the right leads ultimately to San Nicolás.

To climb **Altavista**, use the middle path and zigzag steeply uphill. The path slips off the ridge and climbs to a rocky gap. Simply continue onwards and note how a couple of paths aim directly for the trig point on Altavista at 1376m (4514ft). Views from that point reveal the rugged ridge leading to San Nicolás, framed on all sides by mountains. There is also a view down to the sea and inland to the mountains in the middle of Gran Canaria.

Retrace steps to the gap with the knife-edge ridge and turn sharp left onto the path for San Nicolás. This is stone-paved at first, then runs as an earth ledge on a steep slope of pines. Zigzag down into a gully overlooking the steep and rocky Barranco Hoya del Laurel. Leave this and later cross another gully, with views down to the forest track used on Walk 11 and beyond to the sea at El Risco. Pass a couple of big outcrops full of little caves, then reach a notch in the ridge for a sudden view of San Nicolás surrounded by mountains. The pines thin out and a luxuriant flowery scrub grows along the rocky crest. The path meanders, rises and falls, and basically plays around along the crest. It is a rugged roller-coaster route and is generally clear throughout. Enjoy the mountain views while walking, but take a little care to spot the line of the path when it becomes vague. Eventually, the path heads left of the ridge and zigzags around the slopes of **Montaña Cueva del Humo**.

A track is crossed above a rocky gully, around 800m (2625ft), overlooking some very remote farm buildings. Follow the continuation of the path around the top of another rocky gully, walking roughly parallel

A rugged path climbs a rocky slope close to the summit of Altavista

Looking down a rocky gully on the way round Montaña Cueva del Humo

to the track. The path rises a little, then runs downhill and cuts across a loop of another track twice. Pass close to a makeshift lean-to near a small water source at **Fuente Salada**. Follow the path around a huge, gently sloping hollow in the mountainside. The path descends gently, then rises a little to reach a gap on the far side at the **Morro de los Pinos**, around 760m (2495ft). Looking back at Altavista, note the sacred Guanche peaks to the right – Roque Bentaiga and Roque Nublo. Looking through the gap takes in San Nicolás, and this is a good stance to oversee the line of descent.

Follow the path downhill. It is roughly boulder-paved at first, then is simply a trodden path with little zigzags and a couple of sweeping loops. Pass a huge red boulder and join a track. Turn left to follow the track downhill, crossing and recrossing a water pipeline. The loops become quite pronounced, and the track is rough and stony underfoot. Pass a sign announcing that you are leaving the Parque Natural Tamadaba. Walk down to a couple of ruined buildings and turn right, then slice down to the left along an old track. This leads between fields and lands on another track. Turn left along the track, then almost immediately curve down to the right on a broken, bouldery slope that needs care. As you drop into a valley, aim to land on a track at the bottom.

Turn left to follow the track down past a few houses, then a road called the Subida de la Cruz leads into a broad and stony *barranco*. Swing left up the *barranco*, through an intersection of tracks, then swing right to leave it. Cross another broad and stony *barranco*, then simply follow the road into **San Nicolás**. When a junction is reached at the end of the road, turn right and head straight for the church and plaza in the centre of town. If you are dashing for a bus, then continue past the church to a roundabout. The bus stop for the northern run to Las Palmas is on the right, while the bus stop for the southern run to Las Palmas is off to the left. San Nicolás offers plenty of shops, bars and restaurants, as well as accommodation if you want to stay for the night or use the town as a base for further walks.

WALK 13
San Nicolás to Tasártico

Distance:	17km (10½ miles)
Start:	San Nicolás
Finish:	Tasártico
Maps:	1:50,000 Military Map Sheets 41-42 and 41-43
Terrain:	Mountainous, with plenty of steep and rocky slopes. Paths are mostly clear to follow, but are rough and stony in places and sometimes exposed.

Before leaving **San Nicolás**, have a word with the taxi drivers outside the church if you want to be collected at the end of the day at Tasártico. You can catch a bus a short way along the road from San Nicolás to Albercón, but there are features of interest along the way if you would rather walk. Follow the road called Calle Dr Fleming out of San Nicolás, and note the commercially

Transport:
Global Bus 38 and 101 serve San Nicolás from Las Palmas, running on southerly and northerly routes respectively. Bus 101 and 115 can be used between San Nicolás and Albercón at the start. Call for a taxi to be collected from Tasártico at the end of the walk.

Refreshments:
Shops, bars and restaurants in San Nicolás. Water can be obtained at Güigüí. There is a small bar at the end at Tasártico.

The mountains rising to the west of San Nicolás are remarkably compact, yet while walking through them you imagine that they stretch forever. An intricate arrangement of spiky summits, steep, rocky ridges and deep-cut valleys make this a most entertaining and interesting range. This walk (see map on p. 77) follows the only practicable through-route, which runs from Albercón, near San Nicolás, over to Güigüí, then over to the little village of Tasártico. At the end of the day, you could walk up the road from Tasártico to El Paso to intersect with a bus back to San Nicolás, but it is better to arrange to be collected at Tasártico, and this can be done by arrangement with a taxi driver from San Nicolás.

grown cactus alongside. The Tourist Information Office is in a mock windmill and there are plenty more mills to be spotted. Look out for the restored Molino de la Ladera and Molino de Viento Los Rodriguez. The Calle Albercón leads through the little settlement of **Albercón**, where the Restaurante Grill La Gañania and Cactusland are located. Look out for a big building, the Asociacion de Vecinos la Milagrosa, with a bus shelter built into it, only 60m (195ft) above sea level. Turn left uphill here, along the Calle Subida Cuermeja, which leads to a school. Continue straight up a dirt road alongside a broad *barranco*. When a tarmac road is reached, keep right to follow it further uphill. A couple of reservoirs stand on the hillside and a narrow path runs between them, last seen crudely signposted for 'Guguy'.

The path is stony, gritty and dusty as it runs uphill. The steep and stony slopes bear only a sparse covering of scrub, sometimes thorny, as well as prickly pear and candelabra spurge. The path levels out and descends, then turns round a little side valley. It passes a little ruin on a terrace, then almost reaches a house surrounded by greenery built on a spur. Follow white-painted arrows and turn left uphill before reaching the house. The path zigzags up scrubby slopes and you can see another house far away to the left. Eventually, the path levels out and passes through a rather fine little *barranco*. The next *barranco* is rather nondescript, while the one after that has a dry waterfall, then the path heads for the bed of the main *barranco*. There is a sudden steep climb, and the path is either boulder-paved or rises in stony zigzags to ease the gradient. Towards the top the path swings to the right and almost levels out, passing rocks that bristle with lichen. An airy gap called the Degollada del Peñon Bermejo is reached on a narrow rocky ridge at 693m (2274ft). There are views back the way you came, as well as straight down the Barranquillo del Peñon Bermejo, which plunges to the sea. The path swings left through a groove in the rock, passes above a little cave and follows a gently rising terrace of rock, exploiting a soft creamy layer up to

700m (2295ft). A boulder is painted with the words 'Degoya de Güigüi Chico', and views of the mountain ridges are magnificent.

A long and rugged mountain trail zigzags down into the **Barranco de Güigüí Chico**. Don't follow any lesser paths to the side or attempt to short-cut any zigzags, as the slopes are very rugged. The scrub on the slopes here is very tall. Further downhill, look out for the unusual columnar rock formations in the little cliffs. Watch carefully for the path while passing through terraces and palms at the bottom of the *barranco*. There may be a trickle of water here, at 350m (1,150ft), and this supplies a busy household as well as all their crops and animals. Pass just below the house and walk straight ahead on the level to continue along the path. The way is narrow, but in good condition, and the children from the house regularly ride their bicycles up and down it. While turning a corner, there is a momentary glimpse down through the mouth of the *barranco* to the Playa de Güigüí. You can catch a couple more glimpses of the sandy beach as the path winds further and further uphill.

Pass through a rocky notch in the ridge called the Lomo de Güigüí, at 500m (1640ft), to see yet more mountain ridges and peaks. Swing left to descend towards the Barranco de Güigüí Grande and pass a rock inscribed 'Caña el Besero'. The slopes are rough and rocky, and the path zigzags down into a steep little rocky valley. Keep heading downhill, and avoid the spur path to the left. Cross the **Barranco de Güigüí Grande**, which is filled with cane and palms, then pass a ruin. The path contours across the valley side to pass another ruin, then zigzags down though dry, exhausted terraces to cross the *barranco* again. The cane and palms in the bed of the *barranco* thin out. The path continues gently downhill, then crosses the *barranco* again, passing below some curious little houses. There is a sign reading '**Playa**', and the path to the beach drops down to the right just before it. Cross the *barranco* and climb towards another curious house, but pass below it. A sandy, bouldery path drops steeply through the mouth of the *barranco* to reach the sandy beach. An arrangement of hosepipes means that a trickle of water is generally available for refreshment. At low tide you can head north from this beach to the next little beach at the Playa de Güigüí, which should be less busy.

Walk back up the sandy, bouldery path and cross the *barranco* to return to the 'Playa' sign. Climb up past a couple of houses, passing a water storage pool hidden among some cane. The path is easy at first, but as it heads into the bouldery *barranco* it looks almost impossible to negotiate. However, the path climbs up to the left and the way is simply steep and gravelly instead of bouldery. At a higher level the path crosses the bouldery bed of the *barranco*, then a series of tight zigzags leads up a bouldery slope. Broader zigzags and a gritty path lead up to some telegraph poles and well away from the *barranco*. The surroundings are mountainous and the zigzags lead up to a cliff, where the path swings left and roughly contours round to the head of the *barranco*. This path is on a very steep slope and is narrow and exposed in places. A final set of little zigzags leads to a narrow, rocky gap at the head of the *barranco*, at 547m (1795ft).

The path and the telegraph poles cross this gap, then the path descends in steep, loose and stony zigzags, flanked by scrub and candelabra spurge. Further down it crosses the rocky bed of the Cañada de Aguas Sabinas. A gentler, gritty path runs along the opposite side of the valley, and there is a view of the little village of **Tasártico** and a number of cultivation tents. Stony zigzags lead down to a dirt road at 180m (590ft), and a sign points out that you are leaving the Reserva Natural Especial Güigüí. Follow the dirt road gently uphill to the village and the Bar Victor is one of the first buildings encountered. If it is closed, then use the cold drinks machine alongside. There is a telephone if you wish to call for a taxi, otherwise you can start the long walk up the road through the valley.

Deep in the Barranco de Güigüí Chico where a solitary dwelling is passed

This route (see map on p. 77) follows a long and winding forest track that can be followed from the little village of El Juncal almost to San Nicolás. Its bendy course is anything but direct, but the ground underfoot is always easy and the ascents are never too steep. In any case, when the track climbs up steep mountainsides, it does so in fairly gentle zigzags. The forest track offers easy access to a remote part of Gran Canaria, but there is a slight catch. The track ends abruptly below a rocky little peak called Viso, and the final descent to San Nicolás is on an exceedingly rough and stony path that needs great care. There is another path that can be used towards the end, described in Walk 15, that allows a descent to El Paso, a snack bar on the Degollada de la Aldea.

WALK 14
El Juncal to San Nicolás

Distance:	32km (20 miles)
Start:	Degollada del Aserrador, above El Juncal
Finish:	San Nicolás
Maps:	1:50,000 Military Map Sheets 41-42 and 42-42
Terrain:	Forested mountainsides and valleys for most of the time, traversed using a long forest road. The final descent is on a very steep and rocky slope where the path is stony and eroded and needs great care.

There are no buses to El Juncal, but a Sunday bus service passes the **Degollada del Aserrador**, above the village, on the way from Maspalomas to Tejeda. To shorten the route slightly, take a taxi at San Bartolomé or Tejeda to El Juncal and thus skip the first part of the route. Walkers leaving the Degollada del Aserrador, at 1350m (4230ft), will see a road sign giving the distance to San Nicolás de Tolentino as 20km (12¼ miles), but the forest track is much longer. The road on the left descends in a broad loop into the valley, then runs down towards El Juncal. The village consists of two parts: first, an upper part consisting of a few houses; then a lower part, where a small church is located. On reaching the church, the road winds down to the left and crosses the valley, then rises gently as a dirt road up among pine trees. If you arrive by taxi, then start walking up the dirt road from 1100m (3610ft).

On the ascent, if the distant views allow, you may see El Teide on Tenerife floating above the sea of clouds far beyond the valley mouth. There are also good views back up the valley to the high mountains. The dirt road passes from the Parque Rural El Nublo into the Reserva Natural Integral Inagua, and reaches the Casa Forestal de Pajonales, which looks like a mini-fortress. Walk straight onwards, passing between two huge boulders, generally contouring across the steep, boulder-strewn, pine-clad slopes of a prominent peak. The dirt road swings round a little valley and rises to a junction at **Morrillo de San Juan** at 1261m (4137ft).

To the right is a broad and clear track with a chain across it. Follow this track uphill a little as it contours across a slope of pines, overlooking a broad area that has been grazed quite bare by goats. The peaks of Morro de la Negra and Montaña Solapos de la Carnicería rise to the left, with Montaña de Sándara ahead. The track climbs and contours part-way round Montaña de Sándara, then a series of dusty zigzags leads up the higher slopes, passing a little wayside shrine. The zigzags end, but the track continues climbing and gradually swings round the upper slopes of **Montaña de Sándara**, around 1500m (4920ft). There are views of the high Cumbre of Gran Canaria, as well as of the peak of El Teide. The track crosses a shoulder of the mountain and descends alongside big outcrops that look like enormous boulders. Sweeping loops take the track down from the crest into a huge amphitheatre. Climb gently across the slope to reach a rocky gap on the far side. Cross this and a series of zigzags gives way to a gentler descent. It can be quite rocky alongside the track, otherwise the walk is actually quite easy. A broad crest is reached and there are views either side between the trees. There is a slight ascent, then the track heads off to the left and cuts across a slope where odd stumps of rock and huge boulders are found among the pines. A junction of tracks is reached further along the crest at 1227m (4026ft), on the Degollada de las Brujas. There is a sparse covering of guelder rose, and little cistus bushes are dotted around.

If there is a desperate need for water, then you can turn left and make a long descent to a building where a

Transport:
Global Bus 18 passes the Degollada del Aserrador, above El Juncal, only on Sundays. Taxis can be hired in San Bartolomé or Tejeda to reach El Juncal, thus shortening the route slightly. Global Bus 38 and 101 run from San Nicolás to Las Palmas.

Refreshments:
Shops, bars and restaurants at San Nicolás only. In case of need, water can be reached by a lengthy detour halfway through the walk.

The little village of El Juncal with forested mountains rising beyond

water tap can be found. To continue with the walk, however, turn right to follow the other track down from the high crest. The track swings right and cuts across the head of the valley, then pursues a most convoluted course down into the Barranco de las Casillas. The pines thin out on the way down through the valley, though there are some older specimens that stand much taller than most. Cistus bushes grow abundantly, and a few old buildings will be noticed. Follow the track across the *barranco* to reach a huddle of ruined buildings sitting on a gentle little gap at 880m (2885ft).

One of these is used as an informal bothy, and if for any reason you think you can't complete this walk in daylight, then bear this in mind.

Turn left at these buildings to follow a track that rises in little loops, then makes a big curve up a forested slope to reach a broad, high crest. Note that there is a chance, at this point, to switch to the descent used on Walk 15, otherwise proceed as follows. The track shifts over the crest, making a little zigzag downhill, then descends gently alongside the rocky little ridge of Viso. If you have plenty of time to spare, then by all means include the rugged ridge walk to the trig point on **Viso**, at 997m (3271ft). The track ends abruptly and the final descent needs due caution and care.

Look carefully to spot a rough and stony path, often only a groove full of stones, that continues down the scrubby slope. A steeper path leads down an eroded creamy-coloured groove. Follow a line of little cairns carefully across a creamy-coloured outcrop of rock, then swing left beneath it on an awkward slope of creamy boulders and stones. The brightness can be intense in full sun, but the rocky slope below is darker. The zigzag path needs care as it is little used, eroded in places, and liberally strewn with stones and boulders. Look carefully for every bend and a sparse line of cairns all the way down. The path eventually drifts to the left, round a bend, exploiting soft and friable layers of green and red rock. It slices beneath a monstrous cliff pitted with caves and holes, the refuge of rock doves. Unseen below is a similar cliff, so do not be tempted to short-cut straight downhill. The path is rather a mess as it descends steeply down a rugged nose, passing a small whitewashed wayside shrine around 400m (1310ft), where you might give thanks for a safe deliverance.

The path lands on a track and you turn right to reach a water storage building. Follow a clear track downhill, passing close to a house and leaving the Parque Rural El Nublo. Walk straight down the track,

A view of the mountains from the lower slopes of Montaña de Sándara

passing between cultivation tents, turning right and left to continue down to a road junction where there is a telephone. Turn right down the Calle de Pinillo, passing the big Coagrisan building. Cross a bridge over a broad *barranco* and turn right at a little plaza along the Calle Monteverde. Walk down past a road junction where there are trees and a telephone. Follow the Calle General Franco, then turn left along Calle N de Caceres. Turn right at the first opportunity, then immediately left at a junction planted with cactus. The Calle Cervantes leads to a mini-roundabout, where you walk straight ahead to reach the main plaza and church. To catch a bus, continue past the church to a roundabout. The bus stop for the northern run to Las Palmas is on the right, while the bus stop for the southern run to Las Palmas is off to the left. **San Nicolás** offers plenty of shops, bars and restaurants, as well as accommodation if you want to stay overnight.

WALK 15
Circuit of Inagua

Distance:	18km (11 miles)
Start/Finish:	Degollada de la Aldea
Map:	1:50,000 Military Map Sheet 41-42
Terrain:	Mountainous, with the **start** and **finish** being particularly steep, rocky and exposed, with the danger of rockfall. The use of hands may be required in places. The middle parts of the route follow easy tracks on forested slopes.

Start on the **Degollada de la Aldea**, which bus drivers know as Cruce Tasártico and most travellers call El Paso, after the wooden snack bar on top of the road pass. The path you follow rises straight from the bus stops on top of the road at 680m (2230ft), but be careful of traffic, as there is a blind bend. The path is rugged, but easy enough at first, crossing a scrubby slope beside a low ridge. Pass a telegraph pole and the tiered ramparts of Inagua tower high above. The path slices off to the left and, while still easy underfoot, it is already on a very steep slope, overlooking hairpin bends on the road below. Not long afterwards, you will need to scramble over boulders and up an inclined rock, then pick up a terrace path across a steep slope between two cliffs. When the flowers are in bloom, it is like walking in a botanical garden. Always be aware of the dangers of rockfalls. There is a short stretch that some walkers will find unnerving, where an overhang and a very narrow path need to be negotiated.

The path begins to climb and, looking back, you will realise that you are still basically on the same level

Travellers who cross the Degollada de la Aldea on their way to and from San Nicolás often marvel at the tiered cliffs of Inagua. Few people realise that there is a path up through the cliffs, as well as an exciting path cutting across one of the higher terraces. This walk (see map on p. 77) climbs up through the cliffs, then uses a series of easy tracks to wander far behind Inagua, crossing a gap and descending to an isolated building. The return route uses the higher terrace path, then comes back down through the cliffs to land back on the main road. Both paths on the face of the mountain require a good head for heights and occasional use of hands.

Looking across the valley to the mountains on the ascent of Inagua

as the snack bar at El Paso. Big boulders lie on a slope of dense scrub, then enormous boulders are passed. Climb up through a little valley thick with vegetation, passing a pinnacle of rock and grotesque blocks. Keep climbing across a gentler scrubby slope, among sparse pines, stepping up onto an angled outcrop of rock to follow a line of little cairns. These lead up to a path on a broad ridge, and there is a track running parallel, around 1000m (3280ft). Turn sharp right and follow the track, which descends gently from the crest and makes a wide curve down across a forested slope. It leads to a gap, where you turn right to pass a huddle of ruined buildings around 880m (2885ft). One of these is used as an informal bothy.

Follow the track across the broad valley and swing right to start climbing uphill alongside the Barranco de las Casillas. The track is most convoluted, and cistus bushes and sparse pines give way to a denser cover of pines as more height is gained. Some of the older pines stand much taller than the rest. The track eventually swings right across the head of the *barranco* to reach a junction of tracks on the Degollada de las Brujas at

1227m (4026ft). Simply cross over this broad gap, where guelder rose and cistus grow on the ground, and follow a clear track down the other side. This track descends in a broad, sweeping loop down the forested slope, then approaches close to a solitary building at 980m (3215ft). This is the **Aula de la Naturaleza**, used as a nature study centre by school groups, though it is remote from habitation. There is a water tap here if needed, as well as a fine view down the valley from the front of the building.

Walk back up the track from the building, bending round to the right, then watch carefully for a path rising steeply to the left. This is a tough ascent in the heat of the day, aiming for a little gap on the skyline around 1180m (3870ft). There is an aerial on a rocky little peak to the left and there is a good ground cover of scrub. The path basically contours across a steep slope dotted with pines, with cliffs above and below. There is a view down to the main road, but no direct way down to it. Mountains are ranged opposite, and across the sea you can spot the conical shape of El Teide on Tenerife. Follow the path round a huge rocky amphitheatre and beware of rockfalls. There is a slight descent on the way round, and the path is narrow and crumbling in places. Climb up the far side and look down on the Degollada de la Aldea far below. There are massive organpipe buttresses of rock above; pines and boulders all around. Climb a little from time to time and eventually you will see part of San Nicolás in the distance. The path suddenly swings right, but keep walking straight on down the ridge, or at least cut down past the tors of rock on the next little peak and walk down a slope covered in cistus. The gradient eases and the pines and cistus begin to thin out. The crest becomes rather bare and rocky, and you will notice a track rising on the right, around 1000m (3280ft).

This is your cue to look over the edge on the left to spot the rather vague path you used to reach the crest earlier in the day. When you spot the little line of cairns, drop down and swing sharply left to start the descent. Step down from the tilted outcrop of rock to follow the path down a scrubby slope with sparse

Transport:
Global Bus 38 crosses the Degollada de la Aldea, serving San Nicolás and Las Palmas.

Refreshments:
There is a small snack bar called El Paso on the Degollada de la Aldea. Water can be obtained from the Aula de la Naturaleza in the middle of the walk.

A path picks its way across a terrace on the higher cliffs of Inagua

pines. The path leads past grotesque blocks of rock and a pinnacle, then heads down through a little valley thick with vegetation. Enormous boulders are passed on a slope of dense scrub. The path descends, then picks its way past an overhang where the path is very narrow. The path continues along a terrace and eventually drops to the right, down an inclined rock and over some boulders. Further along, the path swings to the right and finally drops to the main road. Be careful as you land on a blind bend. Refreshments can be obtained at the wooden snack bar called El Paso, at the **Degollada de la Aldea**, while waiting for a bus.

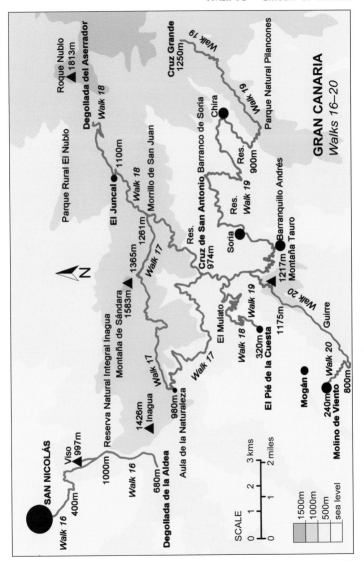

WALK 16
San Nicolás and Viso

Distance:	11km (6½ miles)
Start:	Degollada de la Aldea
Finish:	San Nicolás
Map:	1:50,000 Military Map Sheet 41-42
Terrain:	Mountainous, with several steep and rocky slopes bearing only narrow and sometimes exposed paths. The ascent and descent need care.

Viso rises steep and rocky to the southeast of San Nicolás. It looks like a peak in its own right, but is actually a point on the end of a ridge leading away from Inagua. A direct ascent of Viso would be quite punishing, but this route (see map on p. 99) approaches it in a roundabout way from the Degollada de la Aldea, via a bus service from San Nicolás. On the ascent, a rugged cliff path leads onto the ridge, then, after visiting the summit, a very steep and rocky descent leads back to San Nicolás. Much of this route is rough and rocky, and some parts are exposed and need care.

Start on the **Degollada de la Aldea**, which bus drivers know as Cruce Tasártico and most travellers call El Paso, after the wooden snack bar on top of the road pass. The path you follow rises straight from the bus stops on top of the road at 680m (2230ft), but be careful of traffic, as there is a blind bend. The path is rugged, but easy enough at first, crossing a scrubby slope beside a low ridge. Pass a telegraph pole and the tiered ramparts of Inagua tower high above. The path slices off to the left and, while still easy underfoot, it is already on a very steep slope, overlooking hairpin bends on the road below. Not long afterwards, you will need to scramble over boulders and up an inclined rock, then pick up a terrace path across a steep slope between two cliffs. When the flowers are in bloom, it is like walking in a botanical garden. Always be aware of the dangers of rockfalls. There is a short stretch that some walkers will find unnerving, where an overhang and a very narrow path need to be negotiated.

The path begins to climb and, looking back, you will realise that you are still basically on the same level as the snack bar at El Paso. Big boulders lie on a slope of dense scrub, then enormous boulders are passed.

Climb up through a little valley thick with vegetation, passing a pinnacle of rock and grotesque blocks. Keep climbing across a gentler scrubby slope, among sparse pines, stepping up onto an angled outcrop of rock to follow a line of little cairns. These lead up to a path on a broad ridge, and there is a track running parallel around 1000m (3280ft).

Either walk along or alongside the track while it follows the broad crest. It eventually drops down to the left, so stay high on the crest to continue to Viso. There is only a vague path through the spurge and cistus scrub, and in many places the bedrock is almost like paving slabs. The ridge becomes narrow and rocky before the rather fine rocky peak is reached at the end. **Viso** bears a trig point at 997m (3271ft), which is like a shining white beacon throughout the approach. San Nicolás lies directly below, but on no account should a direct descent be contemplated. Mountains rise inland all the way to the prominent Roque Nublo. Retrace steps back along the ridge, and although a descent to the right is possible to land on the track, it is probably

Viso can be climbed by following its rocky southern ridge to its summit

The path from Viso to San Nicolás drops down steep and rugged slopes

easier to join it where it crosses the crest. After a right turn down the track, there is a little zigzag, then the track heads gently downhill below the crest of Viso.

The track ends abruptly and the final descent needs due caution and care. Look carefully to spot a rough and stony path, often only a groove full of stones, that continues down the scrubby slope. A steeper path leads down an eroded creamy-coloured groove. Follow a line of little cairns carefully across a creamy-coloured outcrop of rock, then swing left beneath it on an awkward slope of creamy boulders and stones. The brightness can be intense in full sun, but the rocky slope below is darker. The zigzag path needs care as it is little used, eroded in places, and liberally strewn with stones and boulders. Look carefully for every bend and a sparse line of cairns all the way down. The path eventually drifts to the left, round a bend, exploiting soft and friable layers of green and red rock. It slices beneath a monstrous cliff pitted with caves and holes, the refuge of rock doves. Unseen below is a similar cliff, so do not be tempted to short-cut straight downhill. The path is rather a mess as it descends steeply down a rugged nose, passing a small whitewashed wayside shrine around 400m (1310ft), where you might give thanks for a safe deliverance.

The path lands on a track and you turn right to reach a water storage building. Follow a clear track downhill, passing close to a house and leaving the Parque Rural El Nublo. Walk straight down the track, passing between cultivation tents, turning right and left to continue down to a road junction where there is a telephone. Turn right down the Calle de Pinillo, passing the big Coagrisan building. Cross a bridge over a broad *barranco* and turn right at a little plaza along the Calle Monteverde. Walk down past a road junction where there are trees and a telephone. Follow the Calle General Franco, then turn left along Calle N de Caceres. Turn right at the first opportunity, then immediately left at a junction planted with cactus. The Calle Cervantes leads to a mini-roundabout, where you walk straight ahead to reach the main plaza and church. To catch a bus, continue past the church to a roundabout. The bus stop for the northern run to Las Palmas is on the right, while the bus stop for the southern run to Las Palmas is off to the left. **San Nicolás** offers plenty of shops, bars and restaurants, as well as accommodation.

Transport:
Global Bus 38 crosses the Degollada de la Aldea, serving San Nicolás and Las Palmas. Global Bus 101 offers a northerly route between San Nicolás and Las Palmas.

Refreshments:
There is a small snack bar called El Paso on the Degollada de la Aldea. There are shops, bars and restaurants at San Nicolás.

This circular walk is suitable for those who have a car to reach the Cruz de San Antonio, near the Embalse de Cueva de las Niñas. The starting point can be approached by road from Ayacata; by road and dirt road from Barranquillo Andrés; or by a long and winding dirt road from El Pié de la Cuesta near Mogán. The route follows a long, winding track around forested mountainsides to reach a solitary building, the Aula de la Naturaleza. Above this building, a series of rough and stony paths can be followed into the mountains (see the map on p. 99). At the end of the circuit another good track leads back down to the Embalse de Cueva de las Niñas, bringing the route to a close at Cruz de San Antonio.

WALK 17
Las Niñas and Ojeda

Distance:	27km (16¾ miles)
Start/Finish:	Cruz de San Antonio
Maps:	1:50,000 Military Map Sheets 41-43, 41-42 and 42-42
Terrain:	Forested mountainsides and rugged ridges. Good tracks are used at the start and finish, while many of the paths in the middle are narrow, rough and rocky in places.

Park near the point where the tarmac and dirt road meet at **Cruz de San Antonio**, at 974m (3196ft). There is another track from this point, with a chain across it, and there is a sign nearby for **Ojeda**. If you reached the start using the dirt roads, then you may be relieved to find that this broad track is mostly a dust-free route! It runs gently downhill across a steep slope of pines and passes a sign for Inagua. A concrete water channel will be spotted, first below the track, then above it. Cross a little bridge over the rocky *barranco* and note the tall, leaning pines nearby. Follow the track gently uphill, then round into the smaller, bouldery Barranco de Mogán. There is a glimpse down the valley to Puerto Mogán. The track rises up around a big hollow in the mountainside to reach stone picnic tables at a tall pine tree at Montaña de Reventon. There is a water tap built into the bank opposite.

The track turns a corner and gradually works its way round the slope, descending slightly across gentler slopes. The pines thin out and there is abundant cistus scrub. Further away to the left, however, are rolling, rocky slopes where very little grows. Views take in jagged mountain summits and the little white shape of the Aula de la Naturaleza is seen far ahead. There is a fine view down into the big Barranco de la Mata, with the Barranco del Medio beyond, and multi-coloured layers of rock exposed below. The track runs gently down to the head of the Barranco de la Mata, crosses it, then rises gently from it. There are some big pines in the *barranco*, and the line of an older trail can be seen below the track. This is still walkable, but rather rough and rocky. Turn a corner to enter and cross the Barranco del Medio, then turn round a rocky nose to reach the **Aula de la Naturaleza** at 980m (3215ft). This is used as a nature study centre by school groups, though it is remote from habitation. There is a water tap here if needed, as well as a fine view down the valley from the front of the building.

Follow the track up from the building, bending round to the right on a slope of pines and cistus. Look across the lower slopes to see a large fenced enclosure. A rather vague and stony path runs towards it, and you need to pick up a path beyond it, leading away from the far side. The path is roughly level across areas of scrub, then crosses gentle, stony, barren slopes. The path enters the upper reaches of the Barranco del Medio. Cross it

Transport:
None

Refreshments:
Water is available from the Aula de la Naturaleza.

Fine mountain views can be enjoyed from the high, forested peaks

Towards the end of the walk, clear and easy forest tracks lead downhill

and aim to keep high, avoiding paths on the lower slopes. Climb from the *barranco* and pines out onto a slope where the path moves across rolling, barren areas of stone, with few pines and only a little scrub. A gentle ascent leads across the upper reaches of the Barranco de la Mata. Turn round a huge hollow in the mountainside, along an easy pine path, with guelder rose on the ground. A junction of paths is reached on a gentle gap. Turn left up a rough, rocky, but gently graded path. Turn round a nose where there is a square stone enclosure with cistus growing all around. Walk downhill a little, then almost along the level, to turn round another rocky nose. Descend easily for a while, then there are boulders lying on the path. Cross a small *barranco*, then follow a crumbling path and squeeze carefully past scrub to reach the rugged Barranco de Mogán.

Cross with care and note that there are two paths on the other side, but both are washed out and not immediately apparent. It doesn't matter whether you take the higher or lower path, as both make their way round the slope into a gentler *barranco* further along. Climb uphill and cross a little gap, then climb a little more and turn a corner. The path is well buttressed, but there is a rough and stony descent. When another path joins from the right, keep left, straight on, though it becomes very rough and stony underfoot. Cross a *barranco* and climb up a series of rugged zigzags strewn with stones and pine cones. Although the path is steep, it finally rises more gently and reaches a broad and rocky gap on a mountain crest between **Montaña de Sándara** and Montaña Solapos de la Carnicería. The altitude is 1,365m (4,470ft).

Cross the broad gap, then the path makes a little zigzag downhill, climbs gently and is quite broad as it crosses the slope of Montaña Solapos de la Carnicería. It becomes stony as it descends to the next gap. Keep to the right-hand side of the forested peak of Morro de la Negra. Rise across a shoulder, then descend to a broad track and follow it down to a chain barrier, where there is a junction with a dirt road on a gap at 1261m (4137ft). Turn right and follow the dirt road down across a slope of pines. The track swings into a valley and rises up the other side, always at a gentle gradient. From a corner there is a view across the **Embalse de Cueva de las Niñas**, as well as to the high mountains at Pico de las Nieves. The dirt road loops downhill, passes below a couple of buildings, and lands on a road. Turn right along the road, gently uphill alongside a rocky *barranco*. There is a bit of a view left to the reservoir dam, then tarmac gives way to the dirt road at **Cruz de San Antonio**.

A series of fine dirt roads is linked to create this route between the isolated village of El Juncal and the lowland village of Mogán. The first dirt road crosses a forested gap and drops down to the Embalse de Cueva de las Niñas (please refer to the map on p. 99). A short walk on tarmac leads to Cruz de San Antonio. At that point, motorists find themselves on a dirt road that they may later have cause to regret.

A long and dusty series of loops and zigzags leads down into a valley, and the uneven surface means that most cars take it at a crawl. As the drivers must focus on the road ahead, they miss the wonderful views along the way, but walkers have time to marvel. When a main road is reached at the bottom, either intercept the San Nicolás bus or walk along the road to Mogán.

WALK 18
El Juncal to Mogán

Distance:	26km (16 miles)
Start:	Degollada del Aserrador, above El Juncal
Finish:	El Pié de la Cuesta
Maps:	1:50,000 Military Map Sheets 41-43, 41-42 and 42-42
Terrain:	Forested mountainsides and steep, rocky valley sides. The entire route is along easy dirt roads, dusty in places, and tarmac roads.

There are no buses to El Juncal, but a Sunday bus service passes the **Degollada del Aserrador**, above the village, on the way from Maspalomas to Tejeda. To shorten the route slightly, take a taxi at San Bartolomé or Tejeda to reach El Juncal and thus skip the first part of the route. A road on the left descends in a broad loop into the valley, then runs down towards El Juncal. The village consists of two parts: first, an upper part consisting of a few houses; then a lower part, where a small church is located. On reaching the church, the road winds down to the left and crosses the valley, then rises gently as a dirt road up among pine trees. If you arrive by taxi, then start walking up the dirt road from 1100m (3610ft).

On the ascent, if the distant views allow, you may see El Teide on Tenerife floating above the sea of clouds far beyond the valley mouth. There are also good views back up the valley to the high mountains. The dirt road passes from the Parque Rural El Nublo into the Reserva Natural Integral Inagua, and reaches the Casa Forestal de Pajonales, which looks like a mini-fortress. Walk straight onwards, passing between two huge boulders, generally contouring across the steep, boulder-strewn, pine-clad slopes of a prominent peak. The dirt road swings round a little valley and rises to a junction at **Morrillo de San Juan** at 1261m (4137ft).

Simply follow the dirt road straight across the gap and down across a slope of pines. The track swings into a valley and rises up the other side, always at a gentle gradient. From a corner there is a view across the Embalse de Cueva de las Niñas, as well as to the high mountains at Pico de las Nieves. The dirt road loops downhill, passes below a couple of buildings, and lands on a road. Turn right along the road, gently uphill

Transport:
Global Bus 18 passes the Degollada del Aserrador, above El Juncal, only on Sundays. Taxis can be hired in San Bartolomé or Tejeda to reach El Juncal, thus shortening the route slightly. Global Bus 38 and 86 run between El Pié de la Cuesta, Mogán and Puerto Mogán for onward connections.

Refreshments:
A few shops, bars and restaurants at Mogán.

A view down the valley from El Juncal reveals distant El Teide on Tenerife

*Looking up through
the valley to the
mountains high above
El Juncal*

alongside a rocky *barranco*. There is a bit of a view left to the reservoir dam, then tarmac gives way to a dirt road at **Cruz de San Antonio** at 974m (3196ft).

The dirt road swings left and is quite bendy as it descends along the upper slopes of Risco Grande. Montaña Tauro towers ahead, further along the rugged crest. A junction is reached with a tarmac road, where you turn right to remain on the dirt road. Bear in mind that the descent along the dirt road is very dusty. If you see a vehicle kicking up a lot of dust, make sure you walk on the dust-free side of the road! Fairly gentle bends take the dirt road down and round a couple of little valleys, passing a few pines. Turn round the slopes of Montaña Chorro de la Burra to reach a hairpin bend and a prominent gate at **El Mulato**. Turn sharp left and enjoy the view from a terrace at the top of a cliff, from where there is a grandstand view of Mogán. A level stretch contours round a little valley, then a series of dramatic zigzags works its way down a shrubby slope. On one of the bends there is a sign for Lomo del Durazno, then another sign for the Barranco del Pino. There is a luxuriantly palm-fringed viewpoint here, where nervous motorists may spend a few moments recovering from their ordeal so far. There may also be an ice cream van parked at this point, dispensing refreshments in the heat of the day.

All of a sudden, at 600m (1970ft), the traffic has a chance to speed up as a corner is turned and the rest of the road is covered in tarmac. However, the road remains bendy and there are still plenty of zigzags to negotiate. The road moves away from the cliffs and zig-zags down into a broad hollow around the Barranco de Mulato. The slopes are bouldery and there are pines all around. After crossing the *barranco*, the road actually climbs for a while and there is some dense scrub on the slopes. After a level stretch, the road zigzags downhill again around the Paso de Ojeda. Enjoy the ever-changing views as the road keeps switching direction, and you can see that the steep, rocky, scrubby slopes are coming to an end. The road swings round some big boulders in the bottom of the valley as it crosses the *barranco* one last time. The last stretch of the road undulates, with palms and luxuriant scrub alongside, passing a few houses before reaching a junction with the main road at **El Pié de la Cuesta**, at 320m (1050ft). Obviously, a German motorist didn't enjoy this descent at all, and has scrawled 'Scheißstrasse' all over the place!

The Bar Restaurant Grill El Draguillo stands near the road junction and there are bus services along the road. If you land here between buses and prefer to keep walking, then simply walk down the road to reach the village of **Mogán**. There are a few shops, bars and restaurants here, as well as an enormous eucalyptus tree in the middle of the road. It is called the Eucalipto Gordo, and buses stop nearby.

WALK 19
Cruz Grande to Mogán

This route links a series of paths, tracks and roads, and thus allows walkers to trek through a variety of landscapes from the mountains around Cruz Grande almost to sea level near Mogán (see map on p. 99). The route is long and potentially tiring. Although some stretches are very easy, there are broad valleys that need to be crossed, and it can take time to drop down into them and climb up the other side. Two large reservoirs are passed on this walk, and a couple of villages along the way offer refreshments. You can arrange to be collected at any point where there is road access, but buses do not serve this route until close to the end near Mogán.

Distance:	40km (25 miles)
Start:	Cruz Grande
Finish:	El Pié de la Cuesta
Maps:	1:50,000 Military Map Sheets 41-43 and 42-43
Terrain:	Forested ridges give way to a gentle valley at Chira, then a bare ridge gives way to a deep and rugged valley at Soria. The last long ascent and descent is along very bendy zigzag roads and dirt roads.

Start at **Cruz Grande**, and note that the bus from San Bartolomé goes through the rocky gap before pulling in to drop off passengers. Walk back through the gap, at 1250m (4100ft), and turn right down a clear track, then keep left, up past a little reservoir. Contour round a slope covered in pines, with a ground cover of guelder rose. Enjoy views of the mountains away to the right, and pass a sign announcing the Parque Natural Pilancones. There is a gradual ascent to a pronounced left bend. At this point, a path descends to the right, marked by parallel lines of stones.

Follow this path downhill, with a little cliff-line to the right, then sweeping zigzags lead down to a path junction. Turn right to descend further, then contour round the slope with good views down the valley. The path climbs up to a gap at the Degollada de Llano Hidalgo, passes beneath a rugged outcrop and keeps climbing, rough and stony underfoot. There are views of the Roque Nublo in the high mountains. The path quickly levels out and contours again, with good views down into the valley and glimpses of the reservoir.

There is also a view from a little gap down to the coast at Maspalomas. The path climbs, contours, descends and then climbs again to reach another gap beneath a prominent rounded peak. There is a narrow path to the left, but keep to the right along the main path, rising and falling around the steep pine-covered mountainside.

Watch out for a clear path descending to the right, with a few stone steps near the top. The path zigzags down to a forest road which is very dusty. You need to go down around only one bend, then drop down beside a concrete water tank. Two pipes run straight downhill from here, and as you follow them and cross from right to left, there are three pipes. Towards the bottom, either follow a track or head straight for the road near the Albergue de Chira and the dam of the Embalse de Chira, around 900m (2950ft). Turn right to follow the winding road, which pulls away from the shore of the reservoir. The Presa Canaria Restaurante up to the right offers food and drink, otherwise keep walking to the little village of Chira.

Follow the road into **Chira** and turn left at a junction, then take the third turn left to continue. There is a building marked 'Bar', but it may well be closed. The undulating concrete road, marked 'Finca Privada', gradually climbs past a few houses and cultivated plots. Keep left at a junction with another concrete road, then keep left to climb past the last house and up onto a broad, barren stony crest at almost 1000m (3280ft). Follow an obvious dirt road, though there is also an option to follow a path part of the way, marked by a line of telegraph poles. When a junction is reached, turn right gently downhill. Walk round a corner and pass below a house, then turn right down a stony track leading above a small rock-bound reservoir. Follow this track onwards further downhill until it ends abruptly around 850m (2790ft).

A narrow path continues, sparsely marked by cairns, but you also have to squeeze through the scrub on the mountainside. Keep your eyes open, as some parts of the path are crumbling. Pass below a huge

Transport:
Global Bus 18 serves Cruz Grande, linking with Maspalomas and Ayacata. Global Bus 38 and 86 run between El Pié de la Cuesta, Mogán and Puerto Mogán for onward connections.

Refreshments:
There is a roadside restaurant at Chira, a bar restaurant at Soria, and a couple of bars at Barranquillo. There are a few shops, bars and restaurants at Mogán.

leaning boulder, then take care, as the path is rather vague across a rocky slope. It leads out onto a point, which reveals below a big hollow full of scrub, with a couple of terraces full of nut trees that you need to reach. Either look carefully for the path or push through the scrub, but either way you need to step down the far side of the terraces. Do this carefully, then cross a bare, rocky *barranco*. Next, follow a narrow, level path along the cliff edge overlooking the *barranco*, and turn round another rocky point. The path is clearer and descends in steep, rough and stony zigzags into a little *barranco* full of nut trees, with a few pines. Watch carefully as the path negotiates terraces at the bottom and drops down to the Barranco de Soria, around 650m (2130ft). There may be a trickle of water here, and a family live and work in this secluded spot.

Turn left after crossing the *barranco*, then go down a rock-step where there is a short rope to hold on to. Keep walking, overlooking the *barranco*, always on the right, no matter how rocky or unlikely the way may seem. When two huge, angular boulders are seen, slice uphill to the right and a good stony path leads straight up to a dirt road. Turn left to follow the dirt road down through the valley to **Soria**. It swings round a side valley, then swings round another valley where there are plenty of palms and towering rock walls. The road is covered in tarmac as it continues to Soria, passing houses and running above a shop called the Viveres Sara. The Restaurante Casa Fernando and another shop offer food and drink in the village, otherwise keep following the road. After turning round a big hollow in the valley side, the next little village reached is **Barranquillo Andrés**, around 650m (2130ft). Here you find the Bar Centro Social Cultural El Montañon, then the road bends round a *barranco* and passes the Viveres Hernadez, both offering food and drink.

Turn right up a road signposted for Tejeda and Mogán. Follow this up past the last houses in the village and start negotiating zigzags on a steep slope of pines. Some of the zigzags can be shortcut if you spot an opportunity to do so. The pines give way to scrub and bare rock as the road climbs higher and higher, but it is also more gently graded towards the top, around 900m (2950ft). A little reservoir can be seen down to the right, guarded by a huge 'No Trespassing' sign. Another sign announces the Parque Rural El Nublo. Also note the path branching off to the left, which climbs towards Montaña Tauro and is used in Walk 20.

A junction is reached with a dirt road, where you turn right to descend to Mogán. Bear in mind that the descent along the dirt road is very dusty. If you see a vehicle kicking up a lot of dust, make

sure you walk on the dust-free side of the road! Fairly gentle bends take the dirt road down and round a couple of little valleys, passing a few pines. Turn round the slopes of Montaña Chorro de la Burra to reach a hairpin bend and a prominent gate at **El Mulato**. Turn sharp left and enjoy the view from a terrace at the top of a cliff, from where there is a grandstand view of Mogán. A level stretch contours round a little valley, then a series of dramatic zigzags work its way down a shrubby slope. On one of the bends there is a sign for Lomo del Durazno, then another sign for the Barranco del Pino. There is a luxuriantly palm-fringed viewpoint here, where nervous motorists may spend a few moments recovering from their ordeal so far. There may also be

A winding track follows a broad and barren crest high above Chira

A dirt road hugs the side of the rocky valley on the way to the village of Soria

an ice cream van parked at this point, dispensing refreshments in the heat of the day.

All of a sudden, at 600m (1970ft), the traffic has a chance to speed up, as a corner is turned and the rest of the road is covered in tarmac. However, the road remains bendy and there are still plenty of zigzags to negotiate. The road moves away from the cliffs and zigzags down into a broad hollow around the Barranco de Mulato. The slopes are bouldery and there are pines all around. After crossing the *barranco*, the road actually climbs for a while and there is some dense scrub on the slopes. After a level stretch, the road zigzags downhill again around the Paso de Ojeda. Enjoy the ever-changing views as the road keeps switching direction, and you can see that the steep, rocky, scrubby slopes are coming to an end. The road swings round some big boulders in the bottom of the valley as it crosses the *barranco* one last time. The last stretch of the road undulates, with palms and luxuriant scrub alongside, passing a few houses before reaching a junction with the main road at **El Pié de la Cuesta**, at 320m (1050ft). Obviously, a German motorist didn't enjoy this descent at all, and has scrawled 'Scheißstrasse' all over the place!

The Bar Restaurant Grill El Draguillo stands near the road junction, and there are bus services along the road. If you land here between buses and prefer to keep walking, then simply walk down the road to reach the village of **Mogán**. There are a few shops, bars and restaurants here, as well as an enormous eucalyptus tree in the middle of the road. It is called the Eucalipto Gordo, and buses stop nearby.

WALK 20
Montaña Tauro

The sheer cliffs of
Montaña Tauro
frown on the little
village of Mogán.
The mountain looks
inaccessible to mere
walkers, but this
route (see map on
p. 99) follows a
fairly easy path lead-
ing onto it, a delight-
fully easy path along
its broad crest, and a
steep and rapid
descent at the end.
All through the
ascent the mountain
looks close to hand,
but it takes a long
time to reach, as
there are so many
zigzags on the road
above El Pié de la
Cuesta. Even if you
get someone to drive
you to the top of the
road it takes time, as
some stretches are
very uneven. Try to
cover this walk on a
clear day early in the
year, when the broad
crest is thick with
colourful and
interesting flowers.

Distance:	18km (11 miles)
Start:	El Pié de la Cuesta
Finish:	Molino de Viento
Map:	1:50,000 Military Map Sheet 41-43
Terrain:	A long zigzag ascent along a tarmac and dirt road. Clear paths lead up forested mountainsides and along a broad crest. The descent is on a steep, narrow and sometimes exposed path needing care in places.

Start at **El Pié de la Cuesta**, at 320m (1050ft), which is within easy walking distance of Mogán, but there are buses passing the road junction near the Bar Restaurant Grill El Draguillo. There is a large sign showing route directions, but offering nothing about the nature of the road ahead. Motorists often set off up this road and receive the shock of their lives at a higher level! The road is tarmac at first, gently undulating past a couple of houses, with palms and luxuriant scrub alongside. The road swings round some big boulders in the bottom of the valley and crosses the Barranco de Mulato. There are a series of zigzags on a steep, rocky, scrubby slope, and you can enjoy the ever-changing views as you climb. Some stretches are level, and there is even a downhill stretch around the Paso de Ojeda. Montaña Tauro, high above the valley, still looks inaccessible to walkers. The road runs across a broad hollow full of dense scrub to cross the *barranco* again, and the slope is covered in boulders and pines. The road continues zigzagging uphill, and the pines begin to thin out as the road shifts out onto the cliffs.

All of a sudden, at 600m (1970ft) on one of the bends, the tarmac ends suddenly and an uneven dirt road continues. Traffic slows to a crawl. Bear in mind that the ascent along the dirt road is very dusty. If you see a vehicle kicking up a lot of dust, make sure you walk on the dust-free side of the road! There is a sign for the Barranco del Pino, and a luxuriantly palm-fringed viewpoint. There may also be an ice cream van parked at this point, dispensing refreshments in the heat of the day.

On another bend there is a sign for the Lomo del Durazno, and a series of dramatic zigzags works its way up a shrubby slope. A level stretch contours round a little valley, then the road runs across a terrace where there is a grandstand view of Mogán. Turn up around a hairpin bend where there is a prominent gate at **El Mulato**. The dirt road climbs round the slopes of Montaña Chorro de la Burra, then runs around a couple of little valleys, passing a few pines. As it climbs further, fairly gentle bends lead up to a junction with a tarmac road. Turn right to follow the tarmac, as signposted for Barranquillo Andrés, and notice how Montaña Tauro doesn't tower so highly now, though its slopes still look steep all around the summit. The road descends a little, then climbs in a series of bends to around 900m (2950ft). A little reservoir can be seen down to the left, guarded by a huge 'No Trespassing' sign. To the right, a path rises from the road.

The path leads easily across a rocky crest and under a pylon line, descending a little to pick a way beneath a rocky peak. After roughly contouring round the slope, a sign is passed for the Monumento Natural Tauro. The path weaves up a slope of pines, then descends gradually for a while. It zigzags uphill again on a steep slope of pines and guelder rose. Watch for a path branching off to the left, which leads to a ruined drystone enclosure on a shoulder of **Montaña Tauro**, offering splendid views inland to the higher mountains. Treat this spur as a diversion, then continue up the main path, which rises across another shoulder of the mountain around 1175m (3855ft).

Transport:
Global Bus 38 and 86 pass El Pié de la Cuesta near Mogán, as well as Molino de Viento on the other side of Mogán at the end of the walk.

Refreshments:
The Bar Restaurant Grill El Draguillo is at the start of the walk. There is only a drinks machine at the end, but for a range of shops, bars and restaurants head for Mogán.

A view from the shoulder of Montaña Tauro reveals Barranquillo Andrés

The descent is like entering a lost valley, and there are no signs of habitation in this rugged enclave. The pines thin out, and even the scrub begins to thin out on the way down a stony slope. The path more or less follows a high crest, then there are pines and cistus scrub as the route runs level for a bit. The descent is gentle on a scrubby slope, leading into another lost valley, keeping to the right-hand side. A ruined building appears, and a peep over a gap beyond reveals the village of Mogán far below, with mountains rising all around and far beyond. Look out for an interesting and unusual little plant called *cardoncillo*, looking like clusters of pale green fingers! Keep to the path skirting across the right-hand side of the valley, and there is another view of Mogán from the next gap. Obviously, when you look over the cliff edge, there is no way down. The path avoids the hill called **Guirre**, which is sparsely covered in pines, and wanders gently across the scrubby, open slopes below the summit. Pass a few pines and note a small drystone-walled enclosure well to the left. Continue along the path, again on a scrubby slope, and it bends to the right, then to the left.

While taking the left bend, look to one side of the path to spot a concealed well that usually offers a little water, if any is needed. The shrubby scrub and flowers on the slope become quite dense and are amazingly colourful early in the year. The path moves close to the cliff edge and skirts around the top of an amphitheatre. It drifts away from the edge into a gentle valley that is amazingly flowery early in the year and attracts vast numbers of butterflies. A right turn leads to a circular drystone enclosure, where the final descent is revealed quite abruptly at 800m (2625ft).

A boulder-paved path picks its way down a cliff, overlooked by a pinnacle of rock, then stout zigzags lead a little further downhill. The path rises and falls along a narrow, vegetated terrace, leading into the amphitheatre that was overlooked from the cliff top. Gravelly zigzags lead down a steep slope of cistus, then the path becomes a little steeper, rougher and stonier as it descends more directly on the scrubby slope further down. Cross a bouldery *barranco* and pass close to a clump of candelabra spurge, then drop down to a point where a track meets a bend on a tarmac road. Follow this road down to a small car park beside the main road at **Molino de Viento** at 240m (785ft).

A prominent windmill has been in sight throughout the descent and it can be studied at close quarters. It was built at the end of 1700, worked until around 1870, then was restored in 1998. Strange sculptures and cactus surround it. There is a bus stop nearby, but the only refreshment is provided by a drinks machine. If anything more is required, or if there is a long time to wait for a bus, then it might be better to walk up the road for a few minutes to Mogán.

A restored 300-year-old windmill at Molino de Viento at the end of the walk

Splendid coastal and mountain views are enjoyed from the Punta Pesebre

FUERTEVENTURA

Fuerteventura is the second largest of the Canary Islands. There is an airport near Puerto del Rosario, the island capital, while ferries berth at Puerto del Rosario, Morro Jable in the south and Corralejo in the north. The island looks rather barren, dry and dusty and is thinly populated. It has the biggest

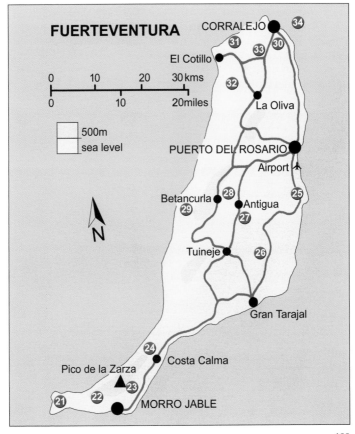

and best sandy beaches of all the Canary Islands and is highly regarded among surfers. Walkers will find plenty of tracks and paths all over the island, but hardly any of them are signposted. Generally, the landscape is bare enough for tracks to be spotted at some distance. Scrub cover tends to be thin, and there are few areas bearing any sort of tree cover. The weather tends to be dry, and the clouds only rarely brush against the tops of the mountains. The highest point is on the mountainous Jandía peninsula and reaches only 807m (2648ft).

Maps of Fuerteventura tend to be vague, so common sense needs to be applied to navigation. There are a handful of fairly popular walks, but the island does not enjoy a high profile among walkers, so much of the landscape remains virtually unknown to most visitors. The following walks fall into three broad areas. There are four varied walks exploring the rugged Jandía peninsula. The central parts of the island are explored in five walks that include short coastal walks, ancient lava flows and easy hill walks. The northern part of the island includes four interlinked walks along the coast and over easy hills, as well as a highly recommended visit to the lovely little desert island of Lobos.

The little village of Puertito de la Cruz as seen from the Punta de Jandía

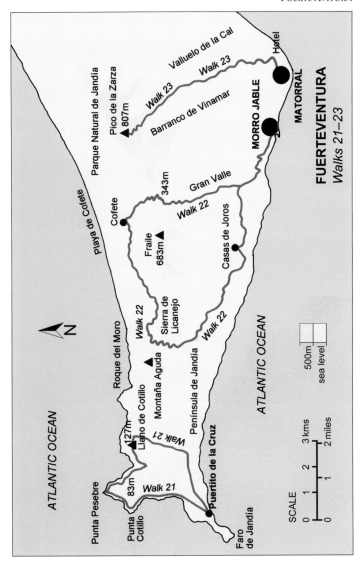

FUERTEVENTURA
Walks 21–23

Hotel

MATORRAL

MORRO JABLE

Valluelo de la Cal

Walk 23

Walk 23

Pico de la Zarza
▲ 807m

Barranco de Vinamar

Parque Natural de Jandia

343m

Gran Valle

Cofete ●

Walk 22

Casas de Joros ●

Fraile
▲ 683m

Sierra de
Licanejo

Walk 22

Playa de Cofete

Roque del Moro

Walk 22

N

Montaña Aguda ▲

Peninsula de Jandia

127m ▲

Llano de Cotillo

Walk 21

ATLANTIC OCEAN

ATLANTIC OCEAN

Punta Pesebre

Punta
Cotillo

83m

Walk 21

Puertito de la Cruz ●

Faro
de Jandia

500m

sea level

SCALE

0   1   2   3 kms

0   1   2 miles

WALK 21
Punta de Jandía

The southwestern tip of Fuerteventura looks well off the beaten track, but there is in fact a good dirt road running all the way there. Every day motorists crawl along the length of the road, have a look at the Punta de Jandía, then drive back again. This route (see map on p. 125) is a scenic walk around the end of the peninsula, featuring a fine cliff coast, a moderate little hill walk and splendid views. The route can be accomplished in a circuit from the tiny village of Puertito de la Cruz, where there are little bar restaurants. It may be a short walk, but when coupled with a long drive along a dirt road (there are no buses beyond Morro Jable, and it is too far to walk) and a break for a meal and a drink, it takes all day to complete the tour.

Distance:	13km (8 miles)
Start/Finish:	Puertito de la Cruz
Map:	1:50,000 Military Map Sheet 45-41/42
Terrain:	Mostly coastal, with good roads, tracks and paths most of the way. There is a short stretch over a hill where the path is vague.

Start at **Puertito de la Cruz**, where there are three little bar restaurants tucked in among a huddle of houses that sit on a stony plain. The tiny village is dominated by a whirling wind turbine, and just down the road is a lighthouse called the Faro de Jandía. Oddly enough, after driving all the way from Morro Jable along a dirt road, the road becomes tarmac near Puertito de la Cruz, though the village streets are gravelly. Two strips of tarmac form a junction alongside the village, opposite the Restaurante Punta de Jandía. One road leads to the Faro de Jandía, while the other is signposted for Punta Pesebre.

You could walk along the road to Punta Pesebre and get there quickly and easily. However, it is worth walking well to the left of the road, along the low cliff-line, but bear in mind that the cliffs are often undercut and you should keep away from the crumbling edge. The road is gently graded, but walking along the cliff edges is more of a roller-coaster route, with lots of little ups and downs. The bedrock is a calcareous sandstone, which is very bright in the full sun and gives the landscape a desert-like look. At the end of the road there is a turning space and a small building capped with a warning light. The **Punta Pesebre** is rough and rocky, with a half-sunken rocky ledge often pounded by the sea. There

Colourful flowers cover desert-like terrain near the village early in the year

Transport:
None

Refreshments:
There are small bar restaurants at Puertito de la Cruz.

are wonderful views along the northern coast of Jandía and on into the central parts of Fuerteventura. From this point, the mountains of Fuerteventura look like little more than a backdrop for a big blue bay.

Continue round the cliff coast either by following the cliff edge with care or by using a vehicle track further inland on the stony plain. The coast offers better views, but the track offers a better ascent to a trig point. The altitude of this rugged little hill is only 83m (272ft), with a view into a rocky bay. Continue along the track, which rises and falls, dropping down into a sandy *barranco* well away from the cliffs. Cross the *barranco* and turn left to follow another rough and stony track uphill. This suddenly rears up very steeply on the rugged hillside, and you should keep just to the right of a sandy little rock gully. Contour to the left beyond the head of this gully, looking ahead to spot a very vague track crossing a rounded stony, sandy hill. There is very little scrub and you aim for a small cairn, where another track is joined. This little hill is the **Llano de Cotillo** and rises only to 127m (417ft). Admire the coastal views for the last time as they will be lost on the descent.

Turn right and follow the track downhill. There are actually several tracks on a steep slope of stones and sand, but they all lead down to a sandy *barranco* where there is only one easy way across. On the other side, walk down a gentle slope of sand, gravel and scrub. The tracks you see ahead are all using a broad and gentle *barranco*, and you may realise that by keeping to the right you will join the dirt road at the foot of the slope closer to the village of **Puertito de la Cruz**. Either turn right along the road, or walk alongside it away from the dust being kicked up by vehicles. The dirt road gives way to tarmac, and the wind turbine is passed before the huddle of houses is reached. You could take a break for a meal and a drink, then maybe take a stroll along the other road to the **Faro de Jandía** afterwards.

WALK 22
Morro Jable and Cofete

Distance:	29km (18 miles)
Start/Finish:	Morro Jable
Map:	1:50,000 Military Map Sheet 45-41/42
Terrain:	Rugged mountain valleys and steep slopes, but there is a good mountain path and a long and gently graded dirt road.

Buses stop just above the centre of **Morro Jable**, and you need to pick your way out of town as if heading for the harbour and ferry services. On the road running down to the harbour, there is a prominent dirt road on the right signposted for the Punta de Jandía and Cofete. There is also a sign for the Parque Natural de Jandía. The dirt road basically contours across the slope, crossing a rugged little *barranco*, then passes below a prominent cemetery on a barren hillside where a few palm trees grow. The dirt road loops downhill to cross another *barranco*, then rises to pass a solitary derelict house. Turn right up a lesser dirt road into the **Gran Valle**, and notice the peculiar prickly euphorbias, known as the Jandía thistle, growing on the slopes nearby. When a couple of cabins and enclosures are reached, follow the track down to the left, passing another sign for the Parque Natural de Jandía. Mountains rise all around this wild valley, and the track follows the gravelly streambed in the bottom. There is a small building off to the right, then later one to the left. Pass through a gap between a stone wall and an old earth dam, then keep right. Be sure to spot a path on the valley side above the gravelly streambed.

The path is flanked by stones and is generally gritty underfoot. It rises gradually, zigzags on the steeper

The Península de Jandía has a mountain range running along its length. Most of the peninsula is protected as the Parque Natural de Jandía. A walk across the rugged range reveals mountain valleys and shapely peaks, while the path underfoot is a remarkable work of engineering. As you will see on the map on p. 125, the path followed on this walk links the remote, ramshackle village of Cofete with Morro Jable, and is so scenic that you might want to follow it both ways. However, the route described here leaves Cofete to follow a very long and winding dirt road over a distant gap and returns to Morro Jable the long way. Vehicles use this dirt road, so if in desperation you needed a quick exit, you could always try hitch-hiking!

Transport:
Tiadhe Bus 1, 4, 5, 9 and 10 serve Morro Jable from points including Puerto del Rosario, Pájara and Costa Calma.

Refreshments:
Plenty of shops, bars and restaurants at Morro Jable. There is a small bar restaurant at Cofete.

slopes towards the head of the valley, and is a joy to walk. Before reaching the high gap at the head of the valley, it crosses a bare and eroded slope. The gap itself is at an altitude of 343m (1125ft) and there are rocky peaks either side. The pyramidal peak of Fraile is to the left, rising to 683m (2241ft), and the village of Cofete lies far below, with seemingly endless sandy beaches stretching either side. An isolated, grand-looking building stands away from the village. It was built by a German who also had the vehicle access road constructed around the mountainside, which you can follow later unless you return via the mountain path. Leave the gap and follow the path along a terrace cut into the rocky slope. A series of zigzags on this slope was recently repaired, so after an initial broken stretch at the top, you will find a splendid path heading down to **Cofete**. Simply turn right at the first ramshackle house and drop down to the main dirt road. If you want to go down to the beach turn right, then left, down a track. If you want to find food and drink, turn left up into the village and head for the big sign reading 'Bar'. Views from Cofete take in the serrated crest of the mountains, often surprisingly green on their northern slopes, with the Pico de la Zarza rising above the grand house on the slopes above the village.

You must now choose whether to retrace the mountain path back to Morro Jable or to take the longer route back via the dirt road. This road is gently graded, but very bendy in places, and it takes a long time to cover. In some parts it is dusty – if the traffic is kicking up a lot of dust, then walk on the dust-free side. The road climbs very gently from Cofete at first, though the slopes it crosses become steeper and more rugged. At one point there is a track dropping down to the right towards the beach, signposted for the Roque del Moro. The slopes become steep, bare and stony, and although the road keeps climbing sometimes there are short descents. After one final ascent on the slopes of **Sierra de Licanejo**, a gap called the Degollada de Agua Oveja is reached, with the pyramidal peak of Montaña Aguda towering above.

A splendid path crosses a rough and rocky slope on the descent to Cofete

There is a parking space at this point, where motorists take a break to enjoy the view, or, if they are on the approach to Cofete, to debate the wisdom of continuing!

The descent from the gap is less scenic than the climb from Cofete, and you soon spot the distant Punta de Jandía. The slopes are bare and stony, with little vegetation, and although the gradient is downhill and easy, there are a lot of loops. By all means shortcut them if you can see a clear way downhill. A junction of dirt roads is reached at the bottom. Puertito de la Cruz is signposted to the right, but turn left for Morro Jable, which isn't signposted. The dirt road is broad, with gentler bends, running gently downhill across barren, arid slopes bearing only a little scrub. Cross the mouth of the Valle de los Mosquitos and rise gently round a slope. A stone is marked for Punta del Viento, indicating a track down to the coast. Keep to the dirt road, running gently down into the Valle de los Escobones, where there is a sign for the Parque Natural de Jandía. Head round and down into the Valle de Jorós, where there are old cultivation plots and derelict buildings, though a few houses are still inhabited. There is a bus shelter here, though there are no bus services!

As the dirt road continues around the broad, stone-strewn slope there are views of the harbour at Morro Jable from time to time. The mountains are set back from the dirt road, though views of the valleys and peaks are good. Pass a sign for the Casa de la Señora, which indicates another track down to the coast. The dirt road passes a junction that was used earlier in the day, at the mouth of the Gran Valle, so all that remains is to retrace steps along the dirt road to return to **Morro Jable**.

WALK 23
Pico de la Zarza

Distance:	17km (10½ miles)
Start/Finish:	Hotel Faro Jandía, Morro Jable
Map:	1:50,000 Military Map Sheet 45-41/42
Terrain:	A long, open crest leading to a bouldery mountain top. A good track and path are used there and back.

Pico de la Zarza is the highest mountain on Fuerteventura at 807m (2648ft). A good track and path run all the way to the summit from the outskirts of Morro Jable, so there is no real difficulty on the ascent. The only difficulty lies in negotiating the road and building developments on the lower slopes. Cloud can cover the peak, and as the views are good from the summit, it makes sense to pick a fine day. This route is offered as a simple there-and-back walk, which could be completed in a morning or an afternoon. Please refer to the map on p.125.

There are bus stops by the Hotel Faro Jandía and you walk along the road to leave **Morro Jable**. Pass Stella Canaris, where there are exotic bird gardens, and reach a roundabout before the Riu hotel. Turn left and follow a road inland alongside the Barranco de Vinamar. A road on the right crosses the *barranco* round the back of the Riu hotel, but do not follow it. Just a little further up the *barranco*, in an area last seen looking like a construction site, turn right and cross the *barranco*. Aim to follow roads ever upwards, crossing a new main road bend, and head higher up the ridge to pick up a track on the slopes above. The track shifts to the right-hand side of the crest, where it has been hacked from a steep slope overlooking the Valluelo de la Cal. Pass a barrier gate and reach a little gap on a narrow part of the ridge. Views down into the ajoining *barrancos* are rather grim, but improve with height. Pass a pylon line on a bare gap beyond, having already spotted the summit far ahead.

The track crosses a slight rise to reach a gentle gap, then climbs uphill by degrees, meandering around on the broad crest. There is very little scrub at first, but at a higher level the track shifts to the left and drops downhill a little, and the slopes alongside are richly vegetated. There are also huge boulders on the slope,

Transport:
Tiadhe Bus 1, 4, 5, 9 and 10 serve Morro Jable from points including Puerto del Rosario, Pájara and Costa Calma.

Refreshments:
Plenty of shops, bars and restaurants at Morro Jable

crusted with lichens. The track passes another gentle gap and zigzags up the higher slopes of **Pico de la Zarza**. When the track ends, a meandering path continues up the bouldery slope to reach the bouldery summit. There is a trig point, a mast and a little wind turbine. Views stretch both ways along the mountainous crest of Jandía and into the middle of Fuerteventura. The little village of Cofete and its broad beaches are seen far below. On a clear day you can expect to see parts of Lanzarote and the mountains of Gran Canaria. Early in the year, the summit is covered in the big yellow, daisy-like flowers of the shrubby Asteriscus. When you have had your fill of the vista, simply turn round and retrace steps to **Morro Jable**.

Pico de la Zarza's steep and rocky northern slopes rise high above Cofete

WALK 24
Costa Calma and El Jable

Distance:	32km (20 miles)
Start/Finish:	Costa Calma
Map:	1:50,000 Military Map Sheet 46-41; 46-42
Terrain:	Mostly gentle slopes, often covered in sand, with a rugged cliff coast and a and sandy beach walk. There are paths and tracks most of the way, but sometimes these can be vague, or easily confused with other paths.

Costa Calma is essentially a resort well known for its sandy beaches, and thus it can be busy by the sea. Head inland to find broad and gently rolling sandy hills, and a rugged cliff coast on the opposite side of the island. The walk moves around the cliff before climbing higher, following a series of sandy tracks towards the mountains. Before reaching the jagged peaks of Jandía, you walk down a gentle barranco that leads back across the peninsula to Risco del Paso. Please see the map on p. 136. Sandy beach walks lead to the Hotel Sol Elite Gorriones and back to Costa Calma.

From the bus stops near the Shopping Center El Palmeral at **Costa Calma** cross the road to a tree-planted area. After finding the a way through to another road, facing a stout wall around a large hotel, turn right. Keep left, walking around the wall and following a road down onto the sandy beach. Turn left to walk along the beach, which is fringed with scrub, palms and lots of apartments. Pass a rocky patch to reach the next sandy beach. There is a small cliff at the end of this beach, before which a road leads inland to the front of the Riu Fuerteventura Playa hotel. As buses serve this area, from a tree-fringed roundabout beyond, you could also start the walk at this point .

Turn right at this roundabout and walk a short way up the road to another one to turn left. At the next roundabout, a short way beyond, turn left again to find the Royal Suite Hotel. Keep to the right of the hotel and follow a sandy, stony track away from the town. There is a sign for the Parque Natural de Jandía along the way. Keep to the lowest and clearest track, which rises gradually through a very sandy and stony valley, called the

Cañada de la Cueva. The higher parts of the valley are more rugged and the track keeps to the right. As the head of the valley is undercut calcareous sandstone, keep away from the crumbling edge. When two tracks diverge from the head of the valley, keep to the right, crossing both the broad crest of the peninsula and a track, which slices from north-east to south-west. Stop for a moment here, and look at the layout of the landscape, consider how the original Guanche inhabitants of Fuerteventura divided the island into two territories.

To the left was the small territory of Jandía, while to the right was the larger Maxorata. Follow a sandy track downhill, crossing other tracks and paths. Eventually you drop down a soft and sandy slope to reach the low cliff-line at **Los Boquetes**.

The cliff walk is accomplished using a fine rocky ledge of sandstone

The cliffs are remarkable. The sea pounds the dark, ancient basalt while the boulder conglomerate and calcareous sandstone, lying on top, is eroded and undercut to form strange shapes. Explore a short way to the right along the cliffs until progress is brought to a halt at a rocky bay. Retrace your steps and continue southwest along the cliffs, keeping away from the crumbling sandstone edge. Odd honeycombed boulders and a lovely little sandy beach are passed. At this point there is an easy path sloping upwards from the beach to the top of the cliffs. Take this path if you wish, otherwise continue exploring the lower cliffs. Little clumps of uvillas grow along here, but most of the rock is bare. Further along the shore you can use another more rugged path

Transport:
Tidhe Bus 1, 4, 5, 9 and 10 link Costa Calma with places such as Morro Jable, Pájara and Puerto del Rosario. Some buses serve the Hotel Sol Elite Gorriones

Refreshments:
There are bars and restaurants around Costa Calma. There is also the Chiringuito Bar at Risco del Paso.

leading uphill. Beyond that, the path along the lower ledge of the cliff narrows until progress is finally halted by a deeply-cut rocky bay. Here a little scrambling is necessary to reach the top of the cliffs. Whatever line of ascent you choose, to continue the walk you will eventually have to head for the easier slopes at the top of the cliffs.

From the cliffs drift inland a little to pick up the clearest sandy and stony track that gently climbs uphill. These hillsides around El Jable are strewn with sand and stones and the scrub looks rather patchy and dry. When you reach junction of tracks at a gentle crest, turn right and aim to stay high on the right-hand side of this crest. Some parts of the track are stone-paved, appearing and disappearing as wind-blown sand allows, whilst other parts are soft, sandy stretches. These are heavy going underfoot but may be avoided by walking on the sides of the track where there are harder patches of shell-sand. The altitude is around 200m (655ft). Though partly obscured by a sandy hill, there are eventually views of the high mountains of Jandía. The track descends and meanders around the slope, eventually passing this sandy hill to reach a gap called the Degollada de Mojones. Take a good look at the mountains before starting the descent.

Carefully follow the track from the gap downhill to the left; some parts are buried in windblown sand. The main road seen below will be reached in due course. It is possible to short-cut some of the initial bends on the track, then follow the bed of a *barranco*. Now decide whether you want to stay in the bed of the *barranco* all the way down to the main road, or use a track that runs alongside on the right, but gradually pulls away from the *barranco* to loop past a small farm at the Casas de Pecenescal. Either way, you need to cross the busy main road to continue. Although buses use this road, as it isn't safe for them to pull in, you will not be able to finish the walk here. The sandy bed of the **Barranco de Pecenescal** leads gently from the main road down to the coast at **Risco del Paso**. Here there is a windsurfing centre and the Chiringuito Bar. Sitting inside this bar is like sitting on the beach; the floor is sandy and the walls are made from woven cane! However, there is also food, drink, and shade from the sun.

There is a choice of two routes along the Playa de Sotavento. Either turn left and hug the coast, or head out to sea and follow a low sandbank between the ocean and a shallow lagoon. Obviously, the latter course depends entirely on the state of the sea and the weather. You will have to wade in places anyway, but the lagoon is very shallow; you'll notice that the water barely reaches their knees of windsurfers who have fallen over! The first route involves passing a rockface, then continuing alongside a scrubby slope. There are a few rock outcrops and little points along the way. The **Hotel Sol Elite Gorriones** is approached as the lagoon becomes full of scrubby little islands, and the shore is fringed with palms and a slope of cactus. A short detour inland leads to a bus stop on the other side of the hotel.

The beach walk and the sandbank walk both lead to another windsurfing centre. Continue along the sandy beach, passing steps that lead up to the Bar Restaurante Villa Esmerelda. When the sandy beach runs into a rocky little cliff, either climb uphill, passing above a little bar and passing close to the big hotel called Playa Esmerelda, or if the water is low and calm, gingerly pick a way around the base of the cliffs. Either way, a dirt track can be picked up beyond the hotel complex. Keep climbing along the road if you want to return to the main road for a bus. When the main road is noticed, look ahead to the Shopping Center El Palmeral. Bus stops are located either side of the round-about just before the shopping centre.

WALK 25
Caleta de Fuste and Pozo Negro

This is a simple walk from one of Fuerteventura's main holiday resorts. It is basically a coastal walk south from Caleta de Fuste to the little village of Pozo Negro. As there are no buses serving Pozo Negro, you should either make arrangements to be collected, or walk back to Caleta de Fuste. Please refer to the map on p. 141. The distance given below assumes you will walk both ways. This walk features the interesting Salinas del Carmen and a whole string of limekilns.

Distance:	24km (15 miles)
Start/Finish:	Caleta de Fuste
Map:	1:50,000 Military Map Sheet 47-40; 47-41
Terrain:	Fairly easy coastal walking, starting on the level but getting hilly towards Pozo Negro. Good paths and tracks are used throughout.

The bus serving Caleta de Fuste stops near a roundabout on the main road. Make your way down to the beach, following an underpass and a sign for the 'Playa'. Along the way there are offers of food and drink and plenty of palm trees. Once you reach the busy beach look across the bay to see the dark structure of the Castillo de Fustes tucked away between all the white-painted buildings. This old fortification that has been spared amid the rampant holiday developments. Turn right to walk alongside, then away from, the sandy beach. As topless bathing on the town beach gives way to full nudity on the rocky shore beyond, Elba hotels spring up south of Caleta de Fuste. The coastal track continues onwards. Tamarisk grows alongside the track for a while, and there are some ruined limekilns. Lime was gleaned by burning the area's calcareous limestone. Further on the rough and stony track passes a huge hotel, where there are some large and interesting restored limekilns on display. Continuing along the track, southwards to Salinas del Carmen, you are never far from a busy main road.

There are two dirt roads in the little village of **Salinas del Carmen**. The one to the right remains high and runs straight through the village and out the other side. The other to the left drops down a little to run

Transport:
Tiadhe Bus 3 is a
regular service
between Puerto del
Rosario and Caleta
de Fuste. Tiadhe Bus
10 is a direct service
from Puerto del
Rosario to Morro
Jable that passes
Caleta de Fuste and
the Salinas del
Carmen.

beside the *salinas*, or salt pans, and round a tiny bay to
end near the Bar Restaurante Los Caracolitas. There is a
narrow, crumbling cliff path leading onwards from the
bar, but as a house bars the way ahead, you have to step
inland to join the other dirt road leaving the village. The
road crosses an arid rise and looks ahead to barren and
stone-strewn hills. However, the road quickly dips
down into a palm-filled valley at **Puerto de la Torre**,
which is an oasis of greenery with a pool, ruins and
another old limekiln.

   Cross the valley to the other side and follow a track
up onto the barren, stony slopes beyond. Go through a
gap in a straggly old fence and stay on the track. It may
be tempting to wander across the stony slopes and follow the cliff-line, but this leads to a crumbling edge
overlooking the Barranco de Majada Honda. Stay on
the track to cross the *barranco*, moving over another
stony slope and down towards the mouth of the little

Refreshments:
There are plenty of
shops, bars and
restaurants at Caleta
de Fuste, a restau-
rant at the Salinas
del Carmen, and a
few bar restaurants
at Pozo Negro.

A series of large restored limekilns are found south of Caleta de Fuste

Barranco de Monte Agudo. The cliffs here look rather good. When the track climbs uphill, switch to a lesser track to the left and cross a small dip, then climb across the stony slope. Again, drop down into another *barranco*, the Barranco Majada de las Cabras, where there is a small cobbly beach and a limekiln.

Climb straight uphill to join the main track again, and follow it over and down into the next broad, barren valley. This is the Barranco de Leandra. Climb up the other side of the valley, keeping left at a fork in the track beside some circular drystone enclosures. As you cross over the hillside at barely 80m (260ft) you get your first glimpse of **Pozo Negro** below. This little village is rather remote and sits above a beach at the end of a road. Follow the track downhill to the road, then walk through the village from one side to the other.

Food and drink are offered at the Restaurante El Rincon de Pozo Negro, Bar Restaurante Los Caracoles and Restaurante Los Pescadores. However, you might like to take your lunch break on the beach, which is either black sand, pebbly, or rocky. On the way back to Caleta de Fuste, you could stop and have your evening meal at the Salinas del Carmen. If you linger over that, then make sure you have a torch to follow the coastal track back to Caleta de Fuste!

Valles de Ortega
240m
Walk 27
Montaña de la Goma ▲
Agua-Bueyes ▲
Walk 27
Tiscamanita
220m
Malpaís Chico
Morro de los Halcones ▲
Walk 27
Llanos de Juan Pablo
La Laguna
160m
▲ Caldera de la Laguna
Walk 26
▲ Caldera de Liria
Llano Prieto
Walk 26
Paisaje Protegido
Malpaís Grande
Casas de Ezquén ●
N
Walk 26
Tequital ●
80m
Monumento Natural de
Los Cuchillos de Vigán
160m
SCALE
0   1   2   3 kms
0   1   2 miles
Arroyo de Cuervo
▲ Vigán
Walk 26
FUERTEVENTURA
Walks 26–27
Las Playitas ●
ATLANTIC OCEAN

WALK 26
Tiscamanita to Las Playitas

Distance:	20km (12½ miles)
Start:	Tiscamanita
Finish:	Las Playitas
Maps:	1:50,000 Military Map Sheets 46-40 and 47-40; 47-41
Terrain:	Easy walking on gently graded tracks in arid, stony surroundings

Everyone who travels the main roads through the middle of Fuerteventura is aware of the windmill at Tiscamanita and the awesome expanse of jagged lava flows on the Malpaís Grande. It is unlikely that many people think of walking from Tiscamanita and across the Malpaís, let alone continue through the hills to reach the coast at Las Playitas. In fact, the walk is easily accomplished using good tracks throughout (see the map on p. 143). Though it is a pity that a main road was constructed across the Malpaís, formerly a very quiet and unfrequented area, the Bar Restaurante Tequital is a bonus for walkers in this desert-like area!

Tiscamanita is a small village that would pass unnoticed were it not for a prominent windmill just above the road. The attached visitor centre, the Centro de Interpretacion Los Molinos de Tiscamanita, provides information about the windmills. In the middle of the village there is a tiny plaza, with a monument to Manuel Velazquez Cabrera (1863-1916), an early mover for Canarian autonomy. There are also three little bars in the village; the Bar Tio Pepe stands near a crossroads, close to the Calle Velazquez Cabrera. Follow the road heading down towards the *malpaís*. The altitude is around 220m (720ft). While passing a few houses (some of which are in ruins) the road becomes a dirt track. The stone here is remarkably like Cotswold stone; the same stone is also frequently found in drystone walls. Rising steeply beyond the cultivated valley down to the left, thick with aloe vera, is the old volcano of Agua-Bueyes. The walls bounding the dirt road splay apart as you reach a fork in the road.

Bear right and follow a broad track close to a couple more houses and simply pass their access roads. The track diminishes as it runs straight out onto a broad and stony plain, with distant ranges of hills on all sides. Join a clearer track and follow this straight onwards, roughly south-east across a broad and barren goat-grazed wilderness. The track passes beneath a pylon line and heads for a slight gap between two low hills. On your left is the big cindery volcano with quarried gashes down its sides. This is the **Caldera de la Laguna**. It is surrounded by jagged lava flows that spilled across the stony plains. A lower hill rising to the right, the **Caldera de Liria,** is still being quarried, as becomes more apparent further into the walk. A low goat-shed is seen up to the left, but stay on the clearest track to cross the low gap, around 150m (490ft), then drop down onto a lower plain called the **Llano Prieto**.

You are likely to spot sheep, goats, mules and maybe even a camel grazing the thin scrub on the Llano Prieto.

Transport: Tiadhe Bus 1 links Tiscamanita with Puerto del Rosario and Morro Jable. Tiadhe Bus 12 links Las Playitas with Bus 1 and 10 services to Puerto del Rosario and Morro Jable

Refreshments: A few bar restaurants at Tiscamanita and Las Playitas, with the Bar Restaurante Tequital in the middle

The windmill at the little museum at Tiscamanita

145

The only farmstead in sight is the diminutive Cortijo de los Arrabales. Follow the track and you will be aware of a noisy quarry off to the left, with trucks rumbling along an access road. Stay off the access road at first, and use a nearby track that crosses the gravelly plain. The hill directly ahead is another volcano, the Caldera de los Arrabales. When the track joins the quarry access road, you need to walk with due regard for the trucks. It can be dusty sometimes, but the road is periodically sprayed with water to counter this problem. You will see a sign for the Paisaje Protegido Malpaís Grande as you follow the access road across the jagged lava flows. Look out for ground squirrels scurrying for cover among the boulders. The dirt road rises and falls, twists and turns, then eventually the lava flow gives way to gentle, gravelly slopes. Rise to join the busy main road near Km32 at the **Casas de Ezquén**.

Simply cross over the road and turn right. Follow a dusty trail roughly parallel to an electricity line. This leads gradually away from the road, overlooking a goat farm and deep pool, then links with a clear track that heads back to the road. There is another sign here for the Paisaje Protegido Malpaís Grande. Cross over the road and follow another track running alongside, though a small property along the way pushes you up onto the road for a while. Drop off the road again as soon as you spot can, then aim for the **Bar Restaurante Tequital**. Food and drink are offered here, near the Km35 mark on the main road, at only 80m (260ft) above sea level. There are also bus stops beside the road, but the only bus service is an express; if you want to use it then be sure to give a very obvious signal!

Leave the Bar Restaurante Tequital, cross over the road and walk up a short stretch of tarmac road, passing a few of the houses that make up this very scattered village of Tequital. Take a right turn onto a broad dirt road leading up across the lower slopes of the hills and follow it with confidence. It climbs gently passing a little house off to the left, as well as a compound full of quarry machinery to the right. However, these arid

slopes are otherwise open and deserted. The road crosses a little gap on the hillside around 160m (525ft), then descends into the broad and open valley of the **Arroyo del Cuervo**. There are fine views of El Roque, the rocky peak dominating the Monumento Natural de Los Cuchillos de Vigán. The lower part of the valley was obviously once fertile, but now all the plots are exhausted and the windpumps are idle. The dirt road rises to a tarmac road, where a left turn leads to a dead-end at the Faro de la Entallada. Turn right to follow the road down to Las Playitas.

When you reach a junction on the outskirts of **Las Playitas** check how much time you can spare. There is a minibus service along the road linking Las Playitas with Gran Tarajal and other bus services. The minibus doesn't really enter the village, but turns at a bus stop to the left. If you have time, walk down into the village and stroll along a little promenade and visit a couple of bar restaurants overlooking the bay. There are a couple more bars further inland.

The Malpaís Grande is an ancient, rugged lava flow in the middle of the island

WALK 27
Tiscamanita to Valles de Ortega

Distance:	15km (9¼ miles)
Start:	Tiscamanita
Finish:	Valles de Ortega
Maps:	1:50,000 Military Map Sheets 46-40 and 47-40; 47-41
Terrain:	Easy walking on gently graded tracks in arid, stony surroundings

This walk allows you to explore the Malpaís Chico (see the map on p. 143). Tiscamanita offers easy access to the broad, level interior of Fuerteventura. Stony plains and jagged lava flow badlands are easily explored using clear tracks. As well as the ancient lava flows, there are broad areas of red earth that were once pressed into cultivation. Today all you will find are grazing goats, some peripheral areas planted with aloe vera, and the jagged lava flows that are used for training hunting dogs. The walk is almost a complete circuit running from Tiscamanita to Valles de Ortega, and linking with bus services on the main road.

Tiscamanita is a small village that would pass unnoticed were it not for a prominent windmill just above the road. The attached visitor centre, the Centro de Interpretacion Los Molinos de Tiscamanita, tells you all about windmills. In the middle of the village you will find the tiny plaza with a monument to Manuel Velazquez Cabrera (1863-1916), an early mover for Canarian autonomy. There are three little bars in the village; the Bar Tio Pepe stands near a crossroads, close to the Calle Velazquez Cabrera. Head down the road towards the *malpaís*. The altitude is around 220m (720ft). While passing a few houses (some of which are in ruins), the road becomes a dirt road. The stone is remarkably like Cotswold stone, and the same stone is frequently used for drystone walls. The old volcano, Agua-Bueyes, rises steeply beyond a cultivated valley, thick with aloe vera, down to your left. The walls bounding the dirt road splay apart as you reach a fork in the road.

Bear left and follow a broad track down a very gentle stony slope. Pass a few houses down to the left. The surrounding terrain is a broad and barren goat-grazed wilderness. The track passes beneath a pylon line and down into a slight dip. Where another track heads off to the right for the cinder cone called the Caldera de la Laguna, keep straight on along the main track. There are old fields of bare, red earth alongside, scattered with stones and surrounded by crumbling walls and earthen banks. Follow the track across this red landscape at 160m (525ft), which tends to become one big mudflat after rain. Step up onto a lava flow at the far side. Signs announce that the rugged boulderfields of the Malpaís Chico are used as a training ground for hunting dogs.

A junction of tracks is reached at the foot of the mountain **Morro de los Halcones**. Turn left to wander between the margin of the jagged lava flow and the smoother slopes of the mountain. A broad, light-coloured level area is passed, which also becomes a mudflat after rain. The track approaches a goat farm at a gap below the little peak of La Atalayita. Keep well to the right of this, staying on the track to reach another junction, then turn left across the lower slopes of **Montaña de la Goma**. These scrubby slopes rise to the right, while the jagged lava flows of the Malpaís Chico are away to the left. The track rises gently and eventually you see a long, low building surrounded by acres of aloe vera, with dusty plains and ranges of hills far

Transport:
Tiadhe Bus 1 serves Tiscamanita and Valles de Ortega

Refreshments:
There are a few bar restaurants at Tiscamanita and Valles de Ortega.

Broad areas of red earth with the volcano of Caldera de la Laguna beyond

beyond. Turn left at the next junction with a dirt road and walk to another junction with a tarmac road.

When the road junction is reached, simply head straight onwards for the distant village of Valles de Ortega, which is set against a shapely range of hills that are traversed on Walk 28. It is mostly a little used open road with a church well away to the left and some ruins to the right (which are again reminiscent of Cotswold stone). Enter the village of **Valles de Ortega** and rise gently to a junction. You can turn left or right, provided that you continue climbing a little more to reach the main road that by-passes the village at around 240m (785ft). There are a few little bar restaurants, but the Bar Restaurante Casa Perez (situated next to a curious windmill structure) is closest to the bus stop on the main road.

WALK 28
Antigua and Betancuria

Transport:
Tiadhe Bus 1 serves Antigua and Bus 2 serves Betancuria, both ruuning from Puerto del Rosario

Refreshments:
Plenty of bar restaurants in Antigua and Betancuria, with a large restaurant also available at the Mirador Morro Velosa.

Distance:	14km (8¾ miles)
Start/Finish:	Antigua.
Map:	1:50,000 Military Map Sheet 46-39
Terrain:	Hilly, with steep slopes in places, but some good paths, tracks and roads. Some short stretches are pathless.

The bus passes **Antigua** on the main road, so walk into the little town and head for the prominent tower of the church, where there is a shady plaza around 250m (820ft). A road leads away from the tower, down into a little valley, with a view straight ahead to the hills you are about to traverse. You will notice a clutch of masts on top of Morro Janana, which is to the left. A building can be seen on top of Morro Velosa, which is to the right, and in-between you can see a path climbing to a gap where

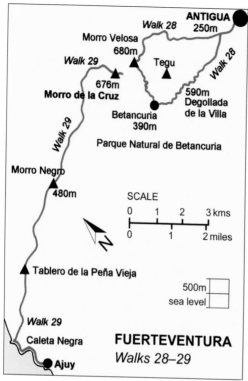

SCALE

| 0 | 1 | 2 | 3 kms |
| 0 | | 1 | 2 miles |

500m
sea level

FUERTEVENTURA
Walks 28–29

Antigua is on the main road through the middle of Fuerteventura and is regularly served by buses. There are only a couple of buses serving Betancuria; a small village couched in a hollow in the hills. Despite its small size, this was once the capital of the island, and it remains a place of quaint cobbled roads, old buildings, and even boasts a ruined Franciscan friary. If you can work around the bus timetables, you can walk over to Betancuria and catch the bus. A better plan, however, is to walk over to Betancuria andthen back over the fine viewpoint summit of Morro Velosa to return to Antigua.

there is an electricity pylon. The gap is the Degollada de la Villa and it will be crossed in due course. First, cross the valley and follow the road uphill past a few palms and houses. There is an open area on the left, with an old, white windmill stump enclosed by a garden wall. Cross this open area, and cross a narrow road, then drop down onto a track. Turn right to follow the track as it rises gradually towards the hills. Avoid turnings to left and right on the last cultivated slopes, but climb straight up the scrubby and sometimes rocky hillside.

Keep to the right at a small block hut and follow the clear track further up the hillside. There are good

151

views back to Antigua, and the skyline beyond is crowded with ranges of hills. There is a sign announcing that you are entering the Parque Natural de Betancuria. If you are wondering why the path is so well-worn, it is not only popular with walkers, but serves as a pilgrim path towards the end of September each year. The path climbs in a series of curves deeply worn into a groove. Towards the top, it slices up to the right across the slope, to reach the gap at the **Degollada de la Villa** at 590m (1935ft). The whole ascent, as well as the gap, is remarkably flowery early in the year. Ignoring the pylon, the view down to the greener landscape below and the huddled village of Betancuria is quite charming.

There are a few stunted pine trees crouching against the hillside on the far side of the gap. A good track leads you down into a big, green hollow, where the hillsides are covered in aloes and all kinds of flowering plants and shrubs. When you reach a tarmac road, the Calle San Buenaventura, walk down it, watching for a path cutting down to the right, so slicing a corner from the road. Ahead, you can see to the church on the other side of the valley. Take any route to it, either following the tarmac road, or cutting across the valley using old cobbled roads.

When you reach the village (at an altitude of 390m (1280ft)) it is worth taking the time to wander around it. Founded by Jean de Béthencourt in 1405, it was the ancient capital of Fuerteventura until 1834. Enjoy the paved and cobbled streets, old houses, the church of Santa Maria, the Museum of Sacred Art, restaurants, bars and ice creams. There are souvenirs aplenty, palm trees and flowers, and, of course, coachloads of visitors. The Restaurante Casa Santa Maria, across the plaza from the church, is like a museum in its own right.

If you want to get the bus back you can find the bus stop on the tarmac road below the church. You could of course walk back to Antigua the same way you came. However, to complete a fine circuit, head for the bus stop below the church, then take a narrow

Descending stony slopes after visiting the restaurant at Mirador Morro Velosa

tarmac road up the valley. This runs roughly parallel to the road that the traffic uses for a while before gradually drifting away from it. The road climbs to provide a view off to the left. The ruined Franciscan friary, with the Ermita de San Diego are seen nearby. The main road below allows regular access to these two places, which are linked by a footbridge. If you try to reach them from the narrow road, you have to use a thin and crumbling path.

Continue up to the end of the narrow road, then climb up a looping track. Always take the highest option at track junctions, passing terraces, water pipes and water storage tanks on the hillside. Eventually, simply climb straight up the rugged, stony and scrubby slope, aiming for the top of the hill. The gradient is steep, but it is not difficult to walk. You may be surprised to reach a road above an old viewpoint, and even more surprised when the road takes you to the summit of Morro Velosa. There is a trig point and cairn at the summit at 680m (2231ft), a notable viewpoint, known as the **Mirador Morro Velosa**. Telescopes allow you to spy on the dry, dusty and thinly populated surrounding countryside. In recent years, however, a huge restaurant has been built on top of the hill. There are two big dining areas, as well as a souvenir shop. If the day is windy, you can eat and drink inside sitting next to big windows to enjoy the view in comfort. Costumed waitresses will serve you here.

Before leaving the viewpoint, take note of the main road snaking down to Antigua. Study the blunt ridge running parallel to it, just to the right, as this is the way you will descend. Also note the track that serves a small building below the summit of Morro Velosa. You can either walk straight down to this track, or double back along the road to a gap in the barrier and follow the track downhill more easily. Either way, walk to the bend just before the building. At that point, turn left and follow a vague track moving steeply downhill and out onto the blunt ridge. This is stony, even rocky in places, but not too hard on the knees. Follow the track downhill, crossing a bit of a hump on the lower stretch, then reach an intersection with a clear dirt road at 372m (1220ft).

Turn right to follow the dirt road downhill. Then from a little valley move uphill, then down and up again, to reach a tarmac road. Turn left to follow the tarmac road gently downhill. It leads past houses and cultivation plots, and later a small school. Keep left at a fork in the road where a garden has been planted. In fact, either road leads back into Antigua, but the left fork crosses the little valley crossed earlier in the day, and climbs straight back to the church. Head straight past the church to the bus stops on the main road. If there is time before the bus arrives you can visit a bar.

WALK 29
Morro de la Cruz to Ajuy

Distance:	16km (10 miles)
Start:	Morro de la Cruz
Finish:	Ajuy
Map:	1:50,000 Military Map Sheet 46-39
Terrain:	Hilly, with steep slopes in places. There is a vague track along the ridges, as well as walls and fences as guides on the higher parts. A short cliff-coast walk leads to Ajuy.

Transport:
Tiadhe Bus 2 runs from Puerto del Rosario to Betancuria and serves the road pass at Morro de la Cruz, but it is better to arrange to be dropped at the start and collected at Ajuy

Refreshments:
There are a few bar restaurants at Ajuy at the end of the walk.

This walk starts at the top of the road running from Antigua to Betancuria. The altitude is already 608m (1995ft) and there is a small viewpoint stance where you can admire the valleys, especially Betancuria, either side of the pass. The ridge leading west from the road is gentle and has a fence running along one side. Pass a TV mast and start climbing steeply, though it doesn't take long to reach a wooden cross and cairn on top of **Morro de la Cruz** at 676m (2218ft). The idea now is to stay as

The Parque Natural de Betancuria consists of rolling hills and dozens of valleys. The hills look gentle enough to offer long ridge walks punctuated by rounded summits, and with care you can indeed select routes like that. Here is a walk that starts high in the hills on the road pass above Betancuria, following a gently rolling ridge all the way down to the sea (please see the map on p. 151). Here amazing rock formations can be visited on the way to the little village of Ajuy. Buses are not really useful on this walk, and it is better if you can arrange to be dropped off on the road pass and collected from Ajuy.

high as possible for as long as possible, so descend northwards down to a gap on a slope that is well vegetated. The gap is actually lower than the road gap where the walk started, dropping to 569m (1867ft) at the Degollada Casas de la Montaña.

The fence that crosses Morro de la Cruz also crosses this gap, but later veers off to the right. There is also a vague vehicle track leading up to the next hill which you need to follow. This vague track leads you like a roller-coaster over a little rise and up to a tumbled stone wall a fence running parallel the wall. Turn left to follow the wall and fence along the blunt crest. Take the time to look down the empty valley leading down to the sea on the other side. Note how the scrub makes the most of the sunny southern side of the wall, where it grows luxuriantly. This hill rises to 673m (2208ft) and is called Morro de la Fuente Vieja. Cross the top and continue along the crest. A fence rises from the left, but keep following the course of the wall and fence together. At the next little summit, which is rather stony, there is a junction of walls, while the fence is located further down the slope. This is the Morro de Gramán at 659m (2162ft) and you turn right here.

While following the wall downhill, look ahead along the broad crest, and then left, to see that this walk heads towards the distant village of Ajuy along the coast. The wall and fence run parallel again, but they also drift to the left of the crest and are no longer useful guides. Around that point, the vague track goes through a wire gate that you cannot untie. Instead use a boulder stile to cross over the fence and continue downhill. The steep slope gives way to a gentle gap where there is an old stone enclosure. Cross a bit of a rise and descend past a chunky cairn before crossing another gentle gap. Looking ahead, the vague track crosses a series of gentle, rounded and stony bumps. One of them bears a concrete base, but it obviously wasn't a trig point since one is reached further along the crest at a height of 480m (1575ft) on **Morro Negro**. Around this point the track almost vanishes, but drop down and follow the

A wooden cross and cairn on top of Morro de la Cruz at the start of the walk

crest further as it reappears on a short, steep and stony slope and is easy to follow further.

When another rounded bump is reached on the stony crest, the track splits and there are two broad crests. Take the one to the right, descending gradually to a stony plain, called the **Tablero de la Peña Vieja**, where there are a number of parallel tracks. All these tracks converge to drop down more steeply into the rugged Barranco de la Peña. There is a small, derelict house here with a palm tree alongside, plenty of tamarisk bushes, a limekiln and an old stone enclosure. Follow the track down the bed of the *barranco* and enjoy the contrast of the fringe of tamarisks after the earlier barren ridge walk. The mouth of the *barranco* leads straight onto a cobbly beach.

There may be several people around as this is a popular site. The Punta de la Peña Horadada features a massive rock stack pierced with a cavernous hole. Depending upon the state of the sea, water sometimes breaks dramatically and unexpectedly through the hole. You only need to look at the surging sea, powerful currents and jagged rocks alternately exposed and submerged, to know that this is a dangerous place to take a dip.

157

A striking rock arch down on the coast at the Punta de la Peña Horadada

However, the scenery is amazing and it is worth spending a while pottering around to take it all in.

To leave, walk back into the *barranco* for a short way, then turn right to follow a cairned path uphill and along the cliff tops. The path is a bit vague, but offers better scenery than the track further inland. Turn round the huge cliff-bound cove at **Caleta Negra**, but keep away from the dangerous undercut cliff edges. Fine caves can be seen, with steps leading down into them from the far side. Make your way round to the top of these steps, at the Mirador en el Puertito de la Peña. Use the steps to get down into a huge sea cave, unless the day is windy or stormy, in which case it would be inadvisable. The sea has worn out the volcanic rock, leaving a roof of calcareous boulder agglomerate. Beware, as those boulders are waiting to fall, and in some places you can see how the roof has collapsed. There are little stalactites where the lime is being leached from the roof. It is possible to scramble over big slippery boulders to the back of the cave, where the sea has punched a smaller entrance through the rock. There is also another cave alongside that tapers back

from the sea until it is very narrow. The calcareous sandstone was cut from nearby cliffs and loaded onto boats
at these caves.

Walk back up the steps and follow the obvious path
with wooden fencing alongside. The bright sandstone
cliffs are very bright on a sunny day, and you can see
where chunks of the rock have been quarried away.
There is a little point where the soft sandstone is eroded
into peculiar little hollows, and this is often crawling
with visitors. There is a view of the village of Ajuy from
here, and rather oddly, given the amount of bright sandstone all around, the beach is dark. There are a few bar
restaurants offering food and drink.

Walk 30: DUNAS DE CORRALEJO

Distance:	8km (5 miles)
Start:	Around the marker Km19 on the road south of Corralejo
Finish:	Mini Tren Terminus at Corralejo
Map:	1:50,000 Military Map Sheet 46/47-38
Terrain:	Low-level sand dunes with some scrubby areas and no permanent paths.

If you want to spend all day walking on the Dunas de
Corralejo, then by all means follow the sandy beach
south of town, then head back through the dunes further inland. However, the inland dunes are lovely and
wild and it seems a shame to start this walk with a tame
stroll along the beach. The best place to start is around
the **Km19** marker on the road, as the dunes further south
are spiked with rocks. Aim to keep well away from the
road and coast, but not so far inland that you walk off
the dunes and onto the rocky slopes beyond.

The Dunas de
Corralejo stretch
southwards as much
as 8km (5 miles) from
the bustling resort of
Corralejo, and inland
from the sea as much
as 3km (2 miles). It
is like a miniature
desert, with rolling
bare dunes, tufts of
scrub, and no perma-
nent tracks or trails
though it. A walk
through the dunes is
best savoured at first
light or towards sun-
set. See the map on
p.160. Please note
that buses do not
stop on the road
through the dunes, so
either take a taxi
south, or find some-
one to drop you off,
then walk back
through the dunes to
Corralejo.

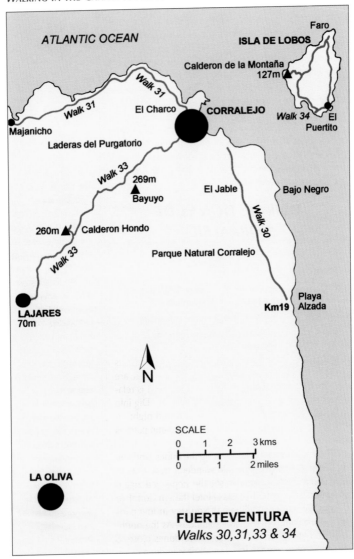

There are no real route directions, except to keep walking roughly northwards through the dunes to return to Corralejo. There are three discernible layers in this intriguing landscape. The base layer is dark basaltic rock. The next layer is a fairly firm calcareous shell sand, formed of the skeletons of minute sea creatures, as well as more easily identifiable snail shells. The top layer is windblown sand, that makes shifting dunes that are heavy going underfoot. In areas where the sand is relatively stable, there is a good covering of scrub. Dig into the sand to discover how moist it is. Humid night air blowing across the dunes often leaves big damp patches on the leeward slopes.

You can meander at will among the dunes, and you may meet an occasional naked wanderer from time to time. Looking ahead you can see the step-sided ziggurat construction of the Tres Islas Hotel though Corralejo remains hidden for some time. If you stay in low parts of the dunes you will see no habitations. As the northern end of the dunes is reached (these dunes close to Corralejo are covered in low scrub), pass under a pylon

Sand and patches of scrub characterise the dunes, with Lobos seen beyond

Transport:
Use a taxi from Corralejo to the Km19 marker on the road south of town. Use the Mini Tren to get back into town.

Refreshments:
There are plenty of shops, bars and restaurants in Corralejo.

The sandy beaches are often busy, but the inland dunes are much quieter. After a blast of wind, you can leave the first set of footprints!

line, well to the left of the big Riu Oliva Beach Hotel. A busy road is reached. With a bit of luck, you will land on this road near a roundabout with a Parque Natural Corralejo sign. Heading straight into town from the roundabout reveals the Apartamentos San Valentin, and opposite is one of the Mini Tren halts, where half-hourly services lead in a huge loop back through **Corralejo**.

WALK 31
Corralejo to El Cotillo

Distance:	23km (14¼ miles)
Start:	Estacion de Guaguas at Corralejo
Finish:	El Cotillo
Maps:	1:50,000 Military Map Sheet 46/47-38
Terrain:	A broad dirt road or sandy track runs all the way along the coast and is gently undulating throughout.

Leave the Estacion de Guaguas, or bus station, at **Corralejo** and walk a short way down the road. Follow a broad dirt road on the left gently downhill past an inlet, called **El Charco del Bristol**. A gentle climb passes close to a desalination plant, and the whole area looks like a desolate wasteland. Pass under a pylon line and continue along the dirt road. The ancient lava flows beside the road are hoary with lichens and feature only a little scrub. The landscape to the left is divided into plots by long drystone walls. The beaches are rocky at first and can be reached by following any of the short tracks down to the right. Lanzarote can be seen across the sea. There are only occasional clapboard dwellings near the road, then the stony wastes are covered by a thin layer of windblown sand. You can see a clutch of small volcanoes rising inland; these can be explored

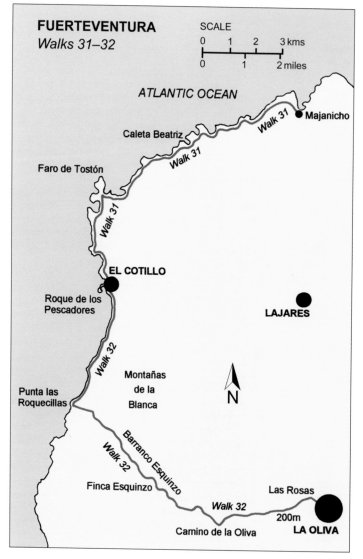

This looks like a very long walk on the map because it is so direct (see the maps on p. 160 and p. 163). It is basically a low-level, easy coastal walk along a clear dirt road or sandy track running all the way from Corralejo to El Cotillo. Walk it in that direction and the scenery gradually improves. There are vast, gentle rocky slopes near Corralejo, with the rocky shoreline being fairly nondescript, but beyond the little village of Majanicho there are sandy beaches and lovely little blue and green bays. Although El Cotillo is growing as a resort, and there are new roads and buildings appearing, the beach walk to the town is quite good and is to be preferred to the road walk.

on Walk 33. Keep following the road, Laderas del Purgatorio, through the stony scrub to reach the **Casas de Majanicho**.

Majanicho has little to offer a passing walker, except the possibility of soft drinks from a cabin. A small *ermita* is dedicated to Nuestra Señora del Pino. The first few houses are separated from the main huddle lying a short way downhill around a small sandy and stony bay. Here there is a junction with another dirt road, which runs directly inland to the village of Lajares. You could follow this and link with the start of Walk 33 to complete a circuit and return to Corralejo. The circuit would measure 26km (16 miles).

To continue, however, follow the dirt road up then downhill to leave the village. The ground underfoot is distinctly brighter and the road runs down a slope of green scrub, then along an expanse of white sand, dotted with drystone windbreak cairns at the Caleta del Hierro. The road climbs a little to turn round a little headland where the old lava flow looks like a boulder-field. There is a little rocky bay below. A short descent leads close to a round, stone goatherd's dwelling. The next building of note is a low, white structure, followed later by a huddle of huts and caravans around a litle low, rocky bay, boarded by a scrap of sandy beach. This is the Caleta Salinas. Further on beyond a long, narrow inlet with a heap of white sand at its head is the **Caleta Beatriz**. Look ahead to see lots of low rocky points, little sandy bays, and the red and white banded **Faro de Tostón**. Inland, the scrubby slopes, divided by drystone walls, give way to distant hills. The terrain becomes very sandy and is sometimes heavy going. There are clumps of scrub and a peppering of dark stones and boulders. The sandy bays get bigger and better, and the last lagoon, the Caleta del Marrajo, protected by a rocky reef, has a shallow sandy floor.

The sandy track wriggles a short way uphill to join a narrow road. You could turn right to follow the road to the Faro de Tostón, but most walkers would be happy to turn left and head straight for El Cotillo. If you do

The Casas de Majanicho lie around on bay between Corralejo and El Cotillo

not wish to walk on the road, follow a sandy and stony track meandering across the hummocky round to the right. There is access to the beach, where at El Caleton you will find the Bar Torino. Here a sandbank holds a sheltered lagoon in place. Pick a way along the beaches and little shore paths to approach **El Cotillo**. This is better than walking along the road! If you have time to spare there are plenty of places offering food and drink. It is worth wandering above the harbour, overlooking **El Roque de los Pescadores**. The actual bus terminus is hidden away near the Hotel Mariquita Hierro, but if you wait behind the bus stop (rather than in front of it) opposite the football pitch at the top of town, you can catch the bus as it leaves town.

Transport:
Tiadhe Bus 8 links Corralejo and El Cotillo. Tiadhe Bus 6 and 7 also link Corralejo and El Cotillo respectively with Puerto del Rosario.

Refreshments:
There are plenty of shops, bars and restaurants in Corralejo and El Cotillo, and also a couple of bars at El Caleton just before El Cotillo.

WALK 32
El Cotillo to La Oliva

Distance:	19km (11¾ miles)
Start:	El Cotillo
Finish:	La Oliva
Map:	1:50,000 Military Map Sheet 46/47-38
Terrain:	Low-level beach and cliff walks, followed by a gentle and gradual ascent inland. Good paths and tracks are used most of the way.

The popular sandy beaches south of El Cotillo give way to a fine cliff-line (see map p. 163). At one point there are steps leading down to a little beach, while a broad, level, stony desert stretches inland. The Barranco de Esquinzo drains this broad area, with its sources in the hills seen far inland. The *barranco* is used occasionally as a vehicle track and is gently graded throughout its course. It can be followed far inland, linking with other tracks to climb gradually to La Oliva. This is a fine, old, sprawling village with a number of interesting old buildings.

Start in **El Cotillo**, at the football pitch at the top of town, and follow the road called the Calle 3 de Abril 1979 to a point overlooking the little harbour. The harbour wall is built out to an islet called **El Roque de los Pescadores**. There are a few bars and restaurants here if you need food or drink at the start, otherwise start walking along the bare and stony cliff tops. There are a few old buildings on the edge of town, including a couple of limekilns and a Martello tower. Cross a little *barranco* before deciding whether to walk along the sandy beach, or climb up the other side to continue. The beach can be busy at times, while the low, rugged slopes just inland are like a roller-coaster ride. Either way, you have to follow the cliff tops when the beach comes to an end. The ground is fairly level, and the path is strewn with stones and dusty-looking scrub. Views over the cliff edge take in a couple of sandy bays, which have no easy means of access, while far inland the rounded hills of the **Montañas de la Blanca** rise to the horizon. Watch carefully to spot one beach that can be reached by a flight of steps, though these are not obvious from the top. If you are prepared to climb back up again you can go down. It is worth walking to the next little headland,

Punta las Roquecillas, for a view both ways along the cliff coast, and to watch rocky sea stacks being pounded by the waves.

Head inland to pass to the left of a solitary fortress-like house. Follow a track directly inland to reach a complex junction of tracks at a small stone enclosure. Follow another obvious track straight inland. It appears to head for the distant mountains seen beyond the Montañas de la Blanca. A few trees can be seen low in the valley, and these will be reached in due course. Keep to the track as it meanders across a stony, scrubby plain with the ruined Casas de Taca away to the right. Follow the shallow Barranco de Esquinzo for a while, before the track drops into it and proceeds upstream along the gravelly bed. There may be a thin trickle of water. The *barranco* is used as a vehicle track and is known as the **Camino de la Oliva**. Tamarisk bushes flank the *barranco* and there is a building surrounded by goat pens. Further upstream there are a couple of old windpumps. When the *barranco* bed is too rocky or bouldery, the track moves alongside it.

A couple more buildings are reached at the **Finca Esquinzo**, and the temptation is to follow a clear track uphill. However, stay low in the bed of the *barranco*, passing mounds of rubble and rising gently uphill. Fig trees will be spotted alongside the *barranco* as a few buildings come into sight. Stay in the *barranco* until a white house surrounded by palms has almost been reached. Just before that point, turn left along another track crossing a confluence of two *barrancos*. The track rises up a broad, stony slope with little scrub. There are views of the steep-sided Montaña Tindaya, with plenty of other hills ranged from right to left. The hill called Oliva stands alone and you can see the track slicing up across its slopes. On the way uphill you can see both an earth dam down to the right, and, at a higher level, step terracing in the valley bottom.

The track crosses a crest over 200m (655ft) at a dump and a ruin to reward you at last with a view of La Oliva. The track is enclosed by walls and fencing and

Transport:
Tiadhe Bus 8 serves El Cotillo and La Oliva from Corralejo. Tiadhe Bus 7 serves El Cotillo from Puerto del Rosario.

Refreshments:
There are plenty of shops, bars and restaurants at El Cotillo. There are a couple of bars at La Oliva.

A fine cliff coast is explored stretching southwards from El Cotillo

reaches a road by-passing the village. Cross over and keep straight on along another road, then turn right to enter the town from **Las Rosas**. Pass the Bar Restaurante Malpey and a football pitch. The Museo del Grano La Cilla is on your right before the junction in the centre of the village. The church is dedicated to Nuestra Señora de la Candelaria. There is also a shop, bar and restaurant across the road. Bus stops are nearby. If there is time to spare, then follow the road signposted for the Casa de Los Coroneles to find a grand, but derelict old house on the outskirts of La Oliva. The Coroneles were military governors of Fuerteventura who, for over a century, got rich at the expense of the peasantry. Another crumbling old building on the outskirts of the village is the Casa del Inglés.

WALK 33
Lajares to Corralejo

Distance:	14km (8¾ miles)
Start:	Lajares
Finish:	Corralejo
Map:	1:50,000 Military Map Sheet 46/47-38
Terrain:	Hilly, with good paths and tracks throughout.

Buses reaching Lajares turn at a mini roundabout, from where you have to walk through the scattered village to reach a crossroads beside a football pitch. The altitude is around 70m (230ft). A signpost indicates a left turn for Playa Majanicho. Follow the road uphill passing a Camel Safari centre to the left at the top of the road. Turn right along a very distinctive track, which is essentially a dirt road with a stone-paved strip along the middle. It climbs gently and slices to the right across the slopes of a rounded cinder cone with quarried flanks. Tucked behind this cone is another rounded hump called Montaña Colorada, towards which the track heads. There is a turning space for vehicles as the track becomes narrower, climbing from a couple of stone pillars. Follow it up through a gap in a drystone wall to reach a junction of two stone-paved paths.

Turn left to follow the path up a gentle, stone-strewn slope to reach another junction. The paved path to the right leads downhill a short way to a restored goatherd's dwelling, which is worth a moment's detour. There are three rooms in this stone-walled structure, with an earth roof on top. There is a hollow cairn outside as well as a stone-walled enclosure. Retrace your steps to the last junction of paths and climb the paved zigzag path leading more steeply uphill. This reaches a surprise viewpoint

This is an interesting walk that wanders over a group of volcanoes between Lajares and Corralejo (see map p. 160). The rounded hillsides are deceptive, but a stone-paved path climbs high on the slopes of Calderón Hondo and reveals a deep and rugged crater. There is also an interesting restored goatherd dwelling on a bleak and stony gap. The undulating track, leading onwards to Corralejo, runs close to the rounded hill called Bayuyo and there is another chance to peep down into a crater. Corralejo is growing all the time and a new, busy road has to be followed back into town. Fortunately, you can link with the course of the Mini Tren service or head straight for the bus station without having to get too far into the bustling town.

169

cut into the rim of a volcanic crater at **Calderón Hondo**. Stand in awe, looking down into the deep crater, with wavy strata exposed in the walls, and look up to the summit on the far side, around 260m (850ft). You could walk round the crater rim with care.

Walk back down the zigzag path, turning right at the last junction and return to the earlier path junction. Turn left to continue across the stony slope and gently down to a junction with a track at a pillar of rock. Turn left, in effect carrying straight on, following the track gently downhill; the slopes above are a complex of interlocked craters best studied from the air! Further downhill there are little houses and fields to the left. Keep straight on along the track, and in any case, tracks leading off to the left are invariably marked as private. The main track climbs towards the rolling whaleback hill of **Bayuyo**, which is the highest hill in this group with its white summit trig point standing at only 269m (883ft). At first you may think that the track is going to climb the hill, however, as it rises and falls, weaves in and out on the hillside, you may think it is going to instead land in a deep crater! It does run close to the crater and a slight climb to the right allows you to peep down into it.

The track appears to descend into the crater on the slopes of Bayuyo

After crossing another rise on the track there is a sudden view ahead to Corralejo, with the islands of Lobos and Lanzarote beyond. Closer to hand are a few goat pens and maybe even a few cows. The track is blighted by fly-tipping for a while and there is a working quarry off to the right. After passing a white water storage building, the track drops to a road. Turn right along this road, then left along a busy main road for Corralejo. You could try short-cutting across stony, pathless scrub to avoid some of the road-walking as the busy dual carriageway into town is unpleasant, but can be covered in a few minutes. The road leads to the bus station where you can link up with the Mini Tren service that runs in a loop around town.

Transport:
Tiadhe Bus 8 serves Lajares from Corralejo and El Cotillo. Bus 7 serves Lajares from Puerto del Rosario and El Cotillo. Bus 6 also offers a link between Corralejo and Puerto del Rosario.

Refreshments:
There are a few bar restaurants at Lajares and many shops, bars and restaurants around Corralejo.

Looking round the steep and rugged crater rim of the Calderón Hondo

171

WALK 34
Isla de Lobos

Distance:	11km (6½ miles)
Start/Finish:	On the pier on Lobos
Map:	1:50,000 Military Map Sheet 46/47-38
Terrain:	Easy coastal tracks and paths with a short hill climb

Do not leave Fuerteventura without visiting the Isla de Lobos (see the map on p. 160). This is the smallest permanently inhabited Canary island and it has the appearance of a desert island. There are daily ferries from Corralejo and a complete lap of Lobos can be accommodated comfortably between the outward and return journeys. Among the interesting things to see are a couple of fine sandy beaches, a miniature mountain, which you can climb, and a couple of restaurants offering food and drink. If tempted to stay longer, take a tent and use the tiny island campsite.

There are two ferries to choose between at Corralejo. One is an ordinary ferry at a budget price, and the other is a more expensive glass-bottom boat. If you get to the harbour early, then the fisherman's bar, the Bar La Lonja de Pescadores is close to hand. Sometimes there is a high demand for trips to **Lobos** but you should ensure that you get the maximum time ashore for walking and don't be tempted with short sailings that only allow a couple of hours.

As you leave the stout concrete pier, note the wheelbarrows chained to the Parque Natural Isla de Lobos sign. These are used by local people to transport goods as no vehicles are allowed on the island. Head straight inland along a clear track, signposted for El Puertito. There is a small campsite to the left of the track. Keep right at a junction of tracks to reach the ramshackle huddle of buildings that constitute **El Puertito**. There are two restaurants, the surprisingly substantial Restaurante El Puertito and the clapboard Restaurante Isla de Lobos. Both restaurants overlook a shallow lagoon.

The track leaving El Puertito drifts inland and may pass a couple of small pools or mudflats, depending upon the water level. There are small, but steep-sided bouldery hills all around. The natural inclination is to drift to the right, back towards the coast, but the track becomes a narrow path leading to a viewpoint. It is

A forest of aloes can be studied at close quarters by making a short diversion

worth the detour, but unless you want to cross the rugged ground beyond, retrace your steps and continue along the track further inland. This crosses a scrubby hollow passing a ruined limekiln to the right.

Transport:
Tiadhe Bus 6 serves Corralejo from Puerto del Rosario. Bus 8 serves Corralejo from El Cotillo. There are two ferries running daily from Corralejo to Lobos.

Refreshments:
The Restaurante El Puertito and Restaurante Isla de Lobos are on the island.

The track runs between two little hills, then crosses a low, scrubby area with a shingle bank well away to the right. The track makes a sweeping zigzag up a slope, passing a small ruin, though a path at this bend provides a short-cut. Further up, notice another track with a paved channel running alongside, heading down to the right. Although this track is a dead-end, it is worth following it to see how water was routed along the channel to an *aljibe*, or underground storage tank. Although the roof has gone, a makeshift lid of driftwood, nets and plastic sheeting covers the water. Keeping to the main track, cross another sandy, scrubby hollow and note another track heading off to the right. This too is a dead-end, leading to a plantation of aloes so dense that it has the appearance of a small forest.

Continue along the main track, moving over a rise, to obtain a view of a tiny wedge of sea ahead, and the lighthouse on Punta Pechiguera on the southern end of Lanzarote. Next, the dumpy little lighthouse at the northern end of Lobos comes into view for a while. Keep to the right at a fork and although the Faro de Lobos can no longer be seen, it will be reached in due course. First, the track wanders down into a sandy hollow where a few abandoned buildings await restoration. Cross the old water channel that once supplied this place. The track reaches a concrete ramp that climbs up to the **Faro de Lobos** on a rounded headland. There are views all round the Isla de Lobos as well as to Fuerteventura and Lanzarote. The area surrounding the lighthouse is used for water collection and storage.

The track heading round the rest of the island is clearer than the one used so far, and if time was pressing you could follow it with confidence back to the pier. It runs between bouldery little hills, overlooks a rocky coast for a moment, then crosses a broad, sandy and scrubby area near the middle of the island. There is no sight of the sea for a while, though if you look carefully, you should spot a sandy path heading off to the right that leads eventually to a grey beach at Caleta del Palo.

The Faro makes a good viewpoint for the rugged eastern coast of Lobos

Of more interest is the next path off to the right, which is dark and cindery, leading to the Caldera de la Montaña. This path stretches across a level, scrubby and stony semi-desert, then rises onto a rough crest. A series of little zigzags lead up to the trig point, and although the altitude is a mere 127m (417ft), it is every bit a mountain and offers a tremendous view. Looking down, the Caleta del Palo is encircled by the ridge of the crater. The whole of Lobos can be seen, threaded by a network of paths and tracks. Northern Fuerteventura and southern Lanzarote loom large and hilly across the sea.

Retrace your steps to the main track, turn right and continue towards the pier or El Puertito. The track continues across the broad scrubland and drops slightly to pass a solitary building where there are a few old fields well to the right. Shortly afterwards, also to the right, is access to a sandy beach and a placid bay at Playa de la Calera. Many people are happy to spend their remaining time on the island here, then return to the ferry.

Moving a little further along the track you can either keep straight on for the pier, or turn left and walk past the little campsite to reach El Puertito. If there is plenty of time to spare before the ferry departs, then a meal can be enjoyed at one of the restaurants.

175

At the start of Walk 35 there are views from the sandy beaches up to Los Ajaches

LANZAROTE

Lanzarote is the fourth largest of the Canary Islands. There is an airport near Arrecife, and ferries berth at Arrecife and Playa Blanca (the latter has fast and regular services to Fuerteventura. The island looks dry and barren, and rainfall is rare, but even among some of the harshest volcanic terrain it is possible to grow all kinds of fruit and vegetables.

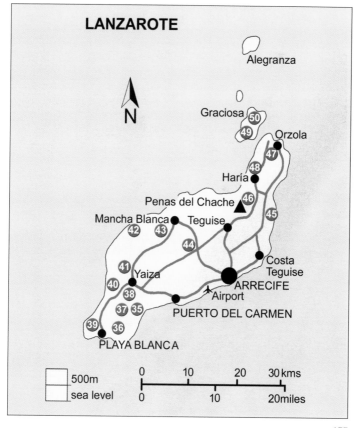

Lanzarote has seen some of the most extensive and prolonged volcanic activity ever recorded in the world, and a huge and fertile part of the island was buried under jagged lava flows between 1730 and 1736, and again in 1824. The highest point on the island, at Peñas del Chache, is a mere 672m (2205ft). Volcanic craters abound on Lanzarote and walkers should have a basic grasp of vulcanism.

Although there are plenty of walking routes around the island, with paths and tracks in the most unlikely places, none of the routes are signposted or waymarked. Bear in mind that access to the Parque Nacional Timanfaya is severely restricted. There is only one walk you can attempt at any time and one other walk that requires a national park guide. The only access to the heart of the national park is on a bus tour. The walks in this book are split between the southern and northern parts of the island. In the south, there are ten walks, many of which take in long stretches of the easily accessible coastline. Several hills are crossed and some of the routes wander across the vast expanses of lava abutting the national park. Another four routes in the north explore the rolling hills and take in more rugged cliff coast walks, including one of the most dramatic on the island.

Looking back along the rugged coastline on the way towards Los Ancones on Walk 45

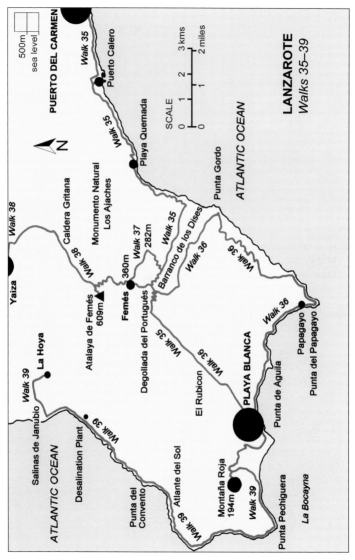

500m
sea level

PUERTO DEL CARMEN

Walk 35

Puerto Calero

Walk 35

Playa Quemada

SCALE

0   1   2   3 kms
0   1   2 miles

Punta Gordo

ATLANTIC OCEAN

LANZAROTE
Walks 35–39

N

Caldera Gritana

Monumento Natural
Los Ajaches

Walk 38

Walk 37
282m

Walk 35

Barranco de los Dises

Walk 36

Walk 36

Yaiza

Walk 38

360m

Femés

Atalaya de Femés
609m

Degollada del Portugués

Walk 35

Walk 36

Papagayo

Walk 36

Punta del Papagayo

La Hoya

Walk 39

El Rubicon

PLAYA BLANCA

Punta de Aguila

Salinas de Janubio

Walk 39

Desalination Plant

ATLANTIC OCEAN

Punta del
Convento

Atlante del Sol

Walk 36

Walk 39

Montaña Roja
194m

Punta Pechiguera

La Bocayna

WALK 35
Puerto del Carmen to Playa Blanca

Puerto del Carmen and Playa Blanca are expanding holiday resorts. Rising between them is a range of shapely hills designated as the Monumento Natural de los Ajaches. This route starts with a coastal walk west from Puerto del Carmen, passing the smaller resort of Puerto Calero and the little seaside village of Playa Quemada, as shown on map p. 179. Beyond there the coast becomes quite bleak and barren, and the hills begin to beckon. Good tracks and paths can be followed high into the hills and down to the broad and stony slopes of El Rubicón. A walk across El Rubicón leads to Playa Blanca.

Distance:	25km (15½ miles)
Start:	Puerto del Carmen
Finish:	Playa Blanca
Maps:	1:50,000 Military Map Sheets 47-36, 47-37 and 48-36
Terrain:	A series of coastal paths and tracks lead easily from Puerto del Carmen to Puerto Calero and on to Playa Quemada. Steeper paths and tracks lead over the hills. Good tracks and vague paths on a gentle, stony slope lead down to a road walk to Playa Blanca.

The walk begins in the middle of **Puerto del Carmen**, where offers of food and drink include everything from fish to English breakfasts. Follow the road downhill as signposted 'Puerto', to reach the church of Nuestra Señora del Carmen by the harbour. Follow a wide flight of steps up the Calle Los Infantes and continue straight along a narrow road. Whether tarmac, brick-paved, or with short flights of steps, the road rising closest to the cliff edge is always called the Calle Los Infantes. There are houses on both sides. Continue along a brick-paved cliff path, enjoying views back over the harbour. Head downhill and straight onwards to leave town and follow paths and tracks across a bare, stony slope. There is a view ahead to the hills of Los Ajaches, with the Punta del Papagayo and neighbouring island of Fuerteventura in the distance. Pass a solitary cliff-top house called Casa Buri, then keep in front of a more substantial walled property. When you come to a rugged path crossing a *barranco*, ensure you cross near the mouth of the *barranco* rather than detouring inland. Cindery paths and tracks continue along the low cliff-line, which is flanked by dusty scrub, to **Puerto Calero**. Just before reaching the yacht-filled marina, follow a diversion uphill and inland to a roundabout.

Turn left at the roundabout. There are two ways of moving through the resort. You can either follow a road past the big Hotel Costa Calero to leave the resort, or take the road turning left down to the marina, though this involves a climb back uphill to continue the route. The Puerto Calero Marina is fringed with palms and is full of gleaming vessels. It is a very Germanic place, with a choice of little bars and restaurants. Angling and cruising trips, diving and submarine safaris are offered from here. Once you have finished exploring the marina climb back uphill past the taxi stand and turn left to pass the big Hotel Costa Calero to leave the resort. Try to keep roughly on the same level as you walk off the end of the road. Avoid the new developments and pick a way past an old windmill stump that has been converted to a house. When you finally drop downhill a little at the edge of the resort, link with a coastal track and follow it on an undulating course towards the hills. **Playa Quemada** can be seen ahead. When you arrive here join a road and head downhill into the village. There is a bus shelter at a road junction, but no bus service. There are three bar restaurants to choose between if you want to take a break at this point.

To leave the village either follow a path over a small headland or, if the sea is clear of the little cliff, crunch along the cobbly beach. Either way you come to a minor valley mouth. Follow a zigzag path climbing uphill on a steep slope to leave the valley, then contour round the slope. Avoid spur paths and keep to the clearest line, then zigzag downhill into the Barranco de la Higuera. Tracks run all over this valley towards the village of Femés, high in the hills. To continue further along the coast, however, simply cross the valley and follow a track uphill past a ruin. There is a small inhabited

Transport:
Arrecife Bus 2 is a regular service between Arrecife and Puerto del Carmen. Bus 6 links Playa Blanca with Puerto del Carmen and Arrecife

Refreshments:
There are plenty of shops, bars and restaurants in Puerto del Carmen and at the end of the walk in Playa Blanca. There are also a few bars and restaurants at Puerto Calero and Playa Quemada.

The coastline is followed past Playa Quemada before heading for the hills

dwelling to the left at the valley mouth, overlooking the cobbly beach. You could follow the track straight up the slope, but it is better to cut off to the left above a ruin, and above the dwelling, to follow the cliff coast. The path leads round a stony slope, then zigzags down to the mouth of the Barranco de la Casita. A strange cactus and palm garden has been planted here, and a cave in the cliff has been imaginatively decorated with all kinds of colourful and interesting flotsam and jetsam. Spend a moment in contemplation.

Walk a short way up the *barranco* and turn left up a narrow path that quickly becomes rather vague on a steep and stony slope. Cairns show the way up a rocky nose and into a little gully, then across a stony slope above the cliffs. When there is a view down into the **Barranco de los Dises**, turn right uphill. There is no path, but the slope is easy, and a vague path appears at a higher leve. A track leads to a junction with another track. Simply keep high on the crest to follow the track over a broad, stony rise and onto a broad saddle. Keep walking straight up the crest, which is now steeper, heading towards the summits of Los Ajaches. There is very little vegetation. When a broad and stony rise is reached, note the tumbled stone enclosure to the right. Drop down onto a broad saddle where there is little trace of a path, then join another path at another tumbled stone enclosure. The zigzag path leads uphill to a shoulder of Pico Redondo; the slopes are like a rock garden early in the year when they are in bloom. Climb over the shoulder at the **Degollada del Portugués**, which is around 450m (1475ft) high. Enjoy the close-up views of the hills and the more distant Playa Blanca and southern end of Lanzarote.

On the descent, there is a fork in the path. You could turn right to Femés if you can arrange to be collected from this little village. Otherwise, turn left to continue the full walk, descending past a goat pen to land on a clear track. Turn right to walk down the track, which descends in huge, well-graded loops on a steep and rocky slope. Take a very good look at the layout of the

broad and rugged area known as El Rubicón, as you will
be walking through it to reach Playa Blanca. Cross over
the busy main road at the bottom of the slope. **El Rubicón**
stretches away into the distance on the other side. There
are three lines of pylons marching off to the left towards
Playa Blanca. Aim for the furthest line of pylons and turn
left, following a vague, stony track for a while. This later
weaves between the two pylon lines furthest from the
road. Keep walking and eventually the lines splay apart,
and at that point you might as well drift towards the main
road across an easy, but pathless plain. Join the road
alongside a water treatment plant and walk straight
through a large roundabout full of palms to continue to
Playa Blanca. The road is called the Avenida de Femés
and leads straight to a bus stop on its way to the port.

WALK 36
Playa Blanca and Los Ajaches

Transport:
Arrecife Bus 6 serves
Playa Blanca from
Arrecife and Puerto
del Carmen.

Refreshments:
There are plenty of
shops, bars and
restaurants at Playa
Blanca, and a cou-
ple of small bar
restaurants at
Papagayo.

Distance:	29km (18 miles)
Start/Finish:	Playa Blanca
Maps:	1:50,000 Military Map Sheets 47-36 and 47-37
Terrain:	Good coastal paths and tracks give way to a fine hill track that climbs gradually over Los Ajaches. Tracks and vague paths lead down a gentle stony slope to a road towards Playa Blanca.

Leave **Playa Blanca** by following the promenade path
around the broad bay. The building developments sometimes cause breaks in the path, but the idea is to piece
together a coastal route out of town. An old tower on the
Punta de Águila has been preserved and incorporated
into a holiday development, but other old buildings carry
notices begging the builders not to destroy them. The

Playa de las Coloradas is an unattractive beach with one final huge building towering above it. After this use any of the paths on the gravelly, scrubby headlands, crossing little *barrancos* and sandy beaches. Keep an eye open to spot the Pozos de San Marcial del Rubicón just inland. These are a series of wells in the bed of a *barranco*, preserved as an archaeological site. Cross the next sandy beach and the headland beyond, then, avoiding the next beach, follow a path up to Papagayo. A handful of little buildings offer food and drink.

Walk round the rugged little headland of **Punta del Papagayo**, and after turning it, there is a chance to drop down onto another sandy beach with a gravel car park just inland. This beach is frequented by nudists. You can either walk along the beach or cross the low cliff-line above it. Further along there is a caravan site with toilets, showers and water taps. Keep walking along the coast until the first of a series of rugged little *barrancos* is encountered. Crossing each and every one of these makes for slow progress, so detour further inland and pick up a clear track on the lower slopes of Los Ajaches.

Avoid all the tracks branching from the main one. Those running towards the coast are dead-ends, while those leading into the hills are of no use. The track makes considerable loops as it crosses a few little *barrancos* and the larger Valle de Juan Perdomo. It climbs over a spur and descends to the Punta Gordo, where there are views around a huge blue bay all the way to distant Arrecife. Los Ajaches rise inland and the next move is to start climbing towards them. Follow the track uphill and inland. It drops a little to cross the Barranco Parrado and again there are junctions with other tracks to avoid. Keep climbing, noticing the drystone ruin off to the right, surrounded by flowers early in the year and by prickly pears at all times. Keep climbing towards a prominent gap at the head of the **Barranco de los Dises**. The track has been hacked from a steep and rocky slope and everywhere looks rather bare due to excessive goat-grazing. There is a goat pen just above the gap, and views are suddenly revealed on the gap at 326m (1070ft). You can

The hills rising inland from Playa Blanca that look so attractive in the morning and evening light have been designated as the Monumento Natural de los Ajaches. This route into Los Ajaches starts by wriggling out of Playa Blanca and its attendant developments. It then enjoys a coastal walk around the Punta del Papagayo. Later, the coastline is cut by too many *barrancos* and it makes sense to head inland, where a track leads high into Los Ajaches. The route is shown on map p. 179. A return to Playa Blanca can be made on the broad, stony slopes of El Rubicón.

A little bar restaurant at Papagayo, before the rocky Punta del Papagayo

see the Playa Blanca and the southern end of Lanzarote, as well as the stony slopes of El Rubicón far below.

The track descends in huge, well-graded loops on a steep and rocky slope. Take a very good look below at the layout of the broad and rugged area, known as El Rubicón, as you will be walking through it to reach Playa Blanca. Cross over the busy main road at the bottom of the slope. **El Rubicón** stretches away into the distance on the other side. There are three lines of pylons marching off to the left towards Playa Blanca. Aim for the furthest line of pylons and turn left, following a vague, stony track for a while. This later weaves between the two pylon lines furthest from the road. Keep walking and eventually the lines splay apart, and at that point you might as well drift towards the main road across an easy, but pathless plain. Join the road alongside a water treatment plant and walk straight through a large roundabout full of palms to continue to **Playa Blanca**. The road is called the Avenida de Femés and leads straight to a bus stop on its way to the port.

WALK 37
Femés Circuit

Distance:	7km (4½ miles)
Start/Finish:	Femés
Map:	1:50,000 Military Map Sheet 47-37
Terrain:	Steep and rugged hillsides, where paths are often narrow, stony and sometimes a little exposed

Start in the middle of **Femés**, an attractive little village that sits high on a gap around 360m (1180ft) in the middle of **Los Ajaches**. Roughly opposite the Bar Restaurante Femés, a narrow tarmac road and farm access road lead quickly up to a couple of concrete buildings on a gap. Walk between these buildings, then follow a path that slices high across the left-hand slopes of Pico de la Aceituna. Take care not to be drawn along another path down to the left, which is actually the path you will follow back to Femés later in the day. The higher path contours across the steep and rocky slope to reach a gravelly gap where a pylon line crosses the slope. At this point, cross over the gap and pick up the path cutting across the right-hand slopes of Pico Redondo. The path is on another steep and rocky slope overlooking the stony wastes of El Rubicón, and it exploits a reddish layer part of the way.

Watch carefully for a junction along the path. Keep left to zigzag a short way uphill and cross a gap called the **Degollada del Portugués** at around 450m (1475ft). Follow the path down a stony, goat-grazed slope. Views on this side of the gap stretch far along the coast to distant Arrecife. You will pass a rocky knoll, then a tumbled stone-walled enclosure further along the crest. The slopes are like a rock garden when they are in bloom

Femés is not particularly well served by buses. You could get there in the afternoon, but you wouldn't be able to leave until early the following morning, and even then, not at weekends. However, if you have a car and can reach the village, there is a fine short circular walk around the peaks of Los Ajaches. Pico de la Aceituna and Pico Redondo rise south of the village and there are narrow and stony paths traversing their steep slopes. Other paths cross the heads of a couple of *barrancos* to return to Femés. For map, see p. 179.

Transport:
Arrecife Bus 5 is an infrequent midweek service to Femés from Arrecife

Refreshments:
There are a few bar restaurants at Femés.

Femés is a small and scattered village on a gap in the middle of Los Ajaches

early in the year. The zigzag path drifts left down into the Barranco de la Casita. Cross over around 220m (720ft) and walk up the other side to reach a shelter beside a water catchment area. This offers welcome shade on a hot and sunny afternoon. Follow the path as it wriggles up a stony slope to reach a broad and bare gap. A path to the right can be used to reach the top of Morro de la Loma del Pozo in a matter of minutes, otherwise keep left to leave the gap at 282m (925ft).

The path descends and cuts across a well vegetated slope. Towards the bottom, in the Barranco de la Higuera, it passes under a pylon line. Keep following the path as it zigzags up an eroded slope at the head of the valley. It eventually reaches the gap above Femés where there are a couple of concrete farm buildings at 408m (1339ft). Simply pass between these and follow the farm access road and a narrow tarmac road back down into Femés. There are three restaurants offering food and drink: the Bar Restaurante Femés, Restaurante Casa Emiliano and Bar Restaurante Balcón de Femés.

The last one is beside a viewpoint, but the views are nothing like as good as those experienced high in the hills.

WALK 38
Femés to Yaiza

Distance:	8km (5 miles)
Start:	Femés
Finish:	Yaiza
Maps:	1:50,000 Military Map Sheets 47-36 and 47-37
Terrain:	Hilly, with good tracks and paths used throughout

Start in the middle of Femés, an attractive little village that sits high on a gap at around 360m (1180ft) in the middle of Los Ajaches. There are three bar restaurants if food or drink are needed at the start of the walk. To start the walk head behind the church, where you will find a patterned brick-paved road makes a loop. Follow it uphill until it starts descending, when you need to head off to the left along a smooth concrete road. This too descends, so take a track up to the left. Avoid the first two left turns from this track. The left turn you want has a chain barrier strung across it with a gap for walkers to get through. This is the access track serving the masts on top of Atalaya de Femés. Crunch along the cindery surface and enjoy the views that open up along the valley. The track zigzags up to a gap where views reveal the valley and hills on the other side, then continues around a crater to reach the summit. There is a trig point on top of **Atalaya de Femés** at 609m (1998ft) but it is dwarfed by the masts that tower overhead. The view stretches from the southern end of Lanzarote, through the stark volcanic central areas, to the hills around and beyond Arrecife.

The prominent peak rising above the village is Atalaya de Femés, is crowned with communication masts. Do not spurn it on this account. It makes a fine viewpoint and it has a volcanic crater near the summit. The rolling crest heading for Yaiza is a joy to walk at the close of the day and overlooks the volcanoes of the Timanfaya National Park (as shown on the map on p. 179). The limited midweek bus service from Arrecife to Femés could prove useful on this walk, provided that there is enough daylight to allow you to walk across the hills to Yaiza in time to catch a late bus.

There are fine views of Los Ajaches on the ridge from Femés to Yaiza

Transport:
Arrecife Bus 5 serves Femés midweek from Arrecife. Bus 6 links Yaiza with Playa Blanca, Puerto del Carmen and Arrecife

Refreshments:
A few bar restaurants at Femés and Yaiza.

Retrace your steps around the crater to return to the gap, then leave the main track and head left along a lesser track to follow the high crest. The track is mostly easy, but take care on some of the short, steep and stony downhill stretches. The village of Uga can be seen ahead, with Yaiza to the left. Further along the crest, the track drifts to the left of **Caldera Gritana**, and the valley descending to Uga is seen to be rather unattractive. A crumbling ruined windmill stump sits on a gap above the valley at 280m (920ft), and a left turn leads straight down a clear track towards Yaiza. There is a level stretch through the fields, then head straight into the village and wait until a big plaza is reached before turning right to reach the main road. If there is time to spare before a bus is due, there are a few bar restaurants offering food and drink.

WALK 39
Playa Blanca to La Hoya

Distance:	23km (14¼ miles)
Start:	Playa Blanca
Finish:	La Hoya
Maps:	1:50,000 Military Map Sheets 47–36 and 47–37
Terrain:	Apart from the initial climb, the gradient is almost level. Good paths and tracks are used most of the time, but some stretches are pathless and covered in stones. The final part is along a road.

The bus to **Playa Blanca** almost reaches the harbour. Don't go down to the sea, but follow the road straight on past the Iberostar Lanzarote Park and Playa Flamingo. The road bends right and heads inland to a junction with a main road. Turn left, then right, as signposted for Montaña Baja and Paradise Island. The road climbs and the Paradise Island hotel is on the right at the top. Turn left along another road signposted for Montaña Baja to climb to a junction. Turn right, even though the road leads only to a mast on the hillside.

Turn right up a dusty, well-trodden path to head for the little volcanic cone of **Montaña Roja**. The path quickly reaches the crater rim, where you can walk either clockwise or anti-clockwise around it. The latter is easier, following a good path round to the trig point on the far side of the crater. The crater slopes support little communities of plants that flower early in the year. From the trig point, at 194m (636ft), there is a view over the sprawling resort of Playa Blanca and the lighthouse on Punta Pechiguera, with Fuerteventura and Lobos beyond. New developments are seen filling a grid network of roads to the west.

The course of this walk can be viewed from a small volcano called Montaña Roja, which offers a fine panorama over the south coast of Lanzarote. There is an immediate contrast between the resort of Playa Blanca and the barren stony slopes all around. Only small clumps of scrub grow on the stony slopes that are brushed by salt spray from breakers on the rocky coast. Eventually, the whole area may be filled with housing, but even if that happens, there will still be a coastal path offering views of the shore line. Please see the map on p. 179.

Transport:
Arrecife Bus 6 serves
Playa Blanca and La
Hoya, linking with
Puerto del Carmen
and Arrecife

Refreshments:
There are plenty of
shops, bars and
restaurants at Playa
Blanca. There is a
restaurant near
La Hoya.

*Montaña Roja is a
small volcanic cone at
the southern end of
Lanzarote*

The centre of Lanzarote is full of shapely volcanic peaks, making little Montaña Roja seem insignificant.

Complete the circuit of the crater, then retrace your steps to start the descent. Watch carefully for a narrow path heading down to the right. Follow this and when it links with roads leading down the built-up slopes of Los Riscos, aim for the main road in front of the hotel called Natura Palace. It is the building with a low-angled pyramidal roof. Turn right along the road, but drop down to a paved coastal path and turn right to follow it towards the lighthouse. You pass sprawling resort buildings surrounded by lush lawns, exotic trees and shrubs; most facilites are private so you should stay on the coastal path. One day this whole area will be filled with developments, but until then there is still a barren plain and a stony path leading to the lighthouse on **Punta Pechiguera**.

A squat little lighthouse stands next to another tall columnar one on the rocky point. Currents are often in conflict here and the wind may stir up big breakers. Little Lobos and the mountains of Fuerteventura are seen across the strait of **La Bocayna**, with ferries running to and fro. Continue through the rock-strewn landscape,

The colourful salt pans at the Salinas de Janubio with a restaurant beyond

hugging the low cliff coast and using any paths or tracks running parallel to the edge. There are building developments along the way and these can be passed on their seaward sides. Don't be tempted along the access roads, which all lead inland. It is usually easy to spot a coastal track linking one place with the next, though sometimes the track is blocked by a mound of rubble.

There are good views back along the cliffs, while inland fine peaks can be seen across the barren stony wastes. A couple of isolated buildings are passed on the way to Punta Ginés, where the path peters out at a fragment of stone wall. The nearest tracks are further inland, so carefully pick a way through the stones and aim for the prominent derelict eyesore of **Atlante del Sol**. If nothing else, the shell of the building offers shade and shelter on an otherwise exposed walk. The ground beyond the building and around Punta Gordo is boulder-strewn and should be taken slowly. Though there is good coastal scenery, it is difficult to walk close to the edge; further inland is easier, but less scenic. There are interesting rocky coves and a prominent rock ledge all the way along the coast. The waves break over this and then the water pours noisily back into the ocean. A curious blowhole might be spotted, where the spray spouts sideways with a curious noise.

A track can be followed past a rocky bay at the **Punta del Convento**. The cliff is undercut and there is a prominent cave, which is best seen once you have passed it, before reaching a trig point at Piedra Alta. Keep following the clear track, maybe detouring for views if you notice the sea spouting dramatically skywards. Pass a desalination plant on the seaward side. The good coastal track turns out to be a dead-end, so leave it early and follow a less clear track just above it. This peters out, but other tracks can be seen ahead and these lead quickly to a car park overlooking the Laguna de Janubio and its salt pans, or *salinas*. A big, dark beach is piled up between the sea and the lagoon. Walk across it to reach a car park on the far side. Unless you want to continue along the coast to El Golfo, turn right and head inland to La Hoya. The road overlooks the salt pans, and there is also the Mirador Salinas Restaurante. The road reaches a roundabout at **La Hoya** where buses pass.

LANZAROTE
Walks 40–43

ATLANTIC OCEAN

Parque Natural de los Volcanes

Walk 42

MANCHA BLANCA

Playa de la Madera

Walk 42

Walk 43

Montaña Caldereta

300m

Visitor Centre

Paletón

458m
Caldera Blanca

Walk 42

Walk 43

Walk 43

Montaña Tingata

Caleta de Ensenada

Parque Nacional Timanfaya

Islote del Hilario

Montañas del Fuego

Ruta de los Volcanes
(Coach tours only)

Montaña Encantada

Ruta de Termesana

Caldera Termesana

Walk 42

Walk 41

N

El Golfo

Walk 40

Walk 42

Vieja Gabriela

Montaña Bermeja

Walk 40

Yaiza

Los Hervideros

Walk 40

La Hoya
Salinas de Janubio

SCALE

0   1   2   3 kms

0   1   2 miles

WALK 40
La Hoya to Yaiza

Distance:	17km (10½ miles)
Start:	La Hoya
Finish:	Yaiza
Map:	1:50,000 Military Map Sheet 47-36
Terrain:	Easy walking along roads, with short paths from time to time

This is a fairly easy road walk, but one that leads through a fascinating volcanic landscape and offers little asides to reveal interesting and dramatic coastal formations along the way (please see the map on p. 195). The route links with bus services at La Hoya and Yaiza, while the little village of El Golfo is ideally placed for a leisurely lunch break. Motorists and tour buses whirl around this loop of road in less than an hour, but aren't really able to fully appreciate the area. There are short walks off the road throughout the route.

Leave the roundabout at **La Hoya** and walk down the road signposted for the Salinas de Janubio and El Golfo. There is a huddle of buildings at the Mirador Salinas Restaurante. If you take a break here, you can look down on the Laguna de Janubio and the grid-pattern of multi-coloured pools that surround it. The pools contain salt water and after slow evaporation they produce salt. The derelict windpumps were used to raise the water from the lagoon to the *salinas*, or salt pans. The lagoon is an important refuge for birds, including varieties of storks and egrets as well as oystercatchers and gulls.

The road leads to a beach car park, but there are much better beaches on the island, so keep following the road as it swings northwards. There are little lay-bys and these usually mark interesting features. At the first one, for instance, there is a fine rock arch where the sea pounds through, and a side-spout feature which often makes the water seething and furious. Further along the road there are more rocky coves, headlands and arches. A car park is signposted for **Los Hervideros**, where you can find a subterranean passageway full of churning water; there are holes allowing people to look down on the scene at various points.

The road squeezes between the little red peak of **Montaña Bermeja** and a little lagoon. The eye is led across masses of jagged lava flows to the Montañas del Fuego in the Parque Nacional Timanfaya. When a road junction is reached, keep left as signposted for Charco de los Clicos. Fangs of rock project from the lower slopes of Montaña de El Golfo. A broken and battered road leads down from a car park to the cove of El Golfo, where a big rock stack is backed by a beach holding a green lagoon in place. The rocky face of Montaña de El Golfo is flashed with rich colours. A red stony ramp of a path leads up to a higher viewing point, from where a path flanked by ropes leads down to a car park, souvenir shop and snack bar. If you walk down through the village of **El Golfo**, there are plenty more bar restaurants, as well as a couple more souvenir shops and a small hotel. The road is a dead-end, so to leave the village you must retrace your steps.

Simply follow the road steeply uphill to pass behind Montaña de El Golfo. Turn left at a road junction, as signposted for Yaiza. The road runs through jagged black lava. Note a track on the left, which is used in Walk 42 to return to the coast. Continuing

Transport:
Arrecife Bus 6 serves La Hoya and Yaiza, linking with Playa Blanca, Puerto del Carmen and Arrecife

Refreshments:
The Mirador Salinas Restaurante is near the start. There are bar restaurants around El Golfo, and a few at the end in Yaiza.

A small green lagoon is couched below cliffs at the Charco de los Clicos

Big breakers pound into the rocky headlands close to the village of El Golfo

towards Yaiza, however, it is possible to walk parallel to the road, on the left, where there is a track of sorts. The road crosses a gap between Pico Redondo, on the left, and **Vieja Gabriela**, on the right. The latter is used as a firing range, which is a pity, as a fine track leads back to La Hoya. These two peaks are entirely surrounded by jagged lava flows that spilled from the Montañas del Fuego. Staying on the road, or on the track just to the left, the road descends and crosses another expanse of broken lava. It rises towards a complex junction with a main road. Walk under the main road, then rise and take the second left to reach **Yaiza**. There are a few bar restaurants on the way through the village, as well as bus stops.

WALK 41
Ruta de Termesana

Distance:	3km (2 miles)
Start:	Below Pedro Perico
Finish:	Caldera Termesana
Map:	1:50,000 Military Map Sheet 47-36
Terrain:	A short, rugged track with a slight climb or descent depending on the direction of the walk

This route starts with everyone leaving the Centro de Visitantes near **Mancha Blanca**. The two minibuses run through the Parque Nacional Timanfaya towards Yaiza, and from there they use two different access points at either end of the **Ruta de Termesana**. Those who are ascending the route will travel out on the El Golfo road before using an access track into the national park. The walk starts at a parking space overlooked by a Timanfaya devil.

The guide leads the way round a cindery hollow to reach a track marked by parallel lines of stones. Do not deviate from this track without the consent of the guide. Pass a big Parque Nacional sign and walk uphill beside ropy *pahoehoe* lava. The guide will point out lava tubes, which resulted when the lava flow formed a solid crust, yet the molten rock inside continued to flow and partly drained away. The whole area is riddled with these tubes, and as the crusts are sometimes very thin, it is dangerous to walk across them. When the tubes collapse they form holes known as *jameos*.

A short walk up the track leads onto the jagged, blocky *aa-aa* type lava, which was more viscous and slow-moving. Off to the left of the track is a small lava lake, while to the right is an eruptive lava bubble which

This is a guided walk, available only to those who book in advance at the Parque Nacional Timanfaya (please see the map on p. 195). Bookings are made so far in advance that you should make enquiries before even setting out for Lanzarote as there are limits on the number of people and days in the week when the walk takes place. The scenery is excellent and the guides offer a thorough grounding in vulcanology and natural history. The only other walking route in the national park is along the coast, covered in Walk 42. The only other way you can experience the scenery is on a coach trip along the Ruta de los Volcanes, also shown on the map on p.195.

Transport:
Minibus transport is provided by the Parque Nacional Timanfaya from the Centro de Visitantes e Interpretacion de Mancha Blanca. Arrecife Bus 15 serves Mancha Blanca from Arrecife

Refreshments:
None, apart from a drinks machine at the visitor centre.

was frozen in the act of bursting. Fig trees have been planted on the cindery slope and are not native to the island. The first plants to colonise the lava are lichens, while spurges, found on the older lava flows around the island, take a thousand years to become established.

A fig tree in a hollow and a palm tree on a higher slope will probably be pointed out. The guide will indicate a large lava flow off to the left that appears to have a canyon carved into it. This was in fact a huge lava tube whose roof finally collapsed. To the right of the track is a relatively flat area of lava, but this is known to contain large tubes. There is a splendid view across to Los Ajaches, which are millions of years old. Contrast that with the mountains in the national park, dating only from the 18th and 19th century!

There is a fine view back to Montaña Encantada, which completely blew out half its cone. Caldera Rajada, on the other hand, is a completely enclosed crater. There are vines on the cindery slopes to the right. As the walk progresses up the cindery track the guide will hand round iridescent lumps of lava for examination, and these must be left behind. There are also some volcanic bombs that were flung from one of the nearby craters. The lava flows that stretched to the coast extended the island by 2 kilometres (1¼ miles), but these bombs could easily be flung ten times that distance.

You may be invited to jump on a level patch of lava and feel the vibrations, as there is a tube not far underground. The walk leads up past fig trees surrounded by circular walls. The walls keep off the wind and airborne salts, but trap the humidity from the air. The track rises onto more blocky aa-aa. To the left there is a drying platform for figs, made from the cindery pumice lying all around. Aim for the mountain ahead, then swing right along a level cindery track. You can go down into a hollow at **Caldera Termesana** and see where farmers dug holes after the eruptions to find the original soil beneath so that they could plant trees.

Leaving the hollow, the track crosses a rise and there are fine views into the heart of the national park, then the track runs down to a barrier gate where the other minibus will be waiting. This short walk will give insights into what makes Timanfaya so special, and it is obvious while studying the fragile nature of the landforms that allowing indiscrimate walking would cause a lot of damage. On the drive along the rugged track to **Yaiza**, you can see the narrow trail that local farmers made over a century ago across the lava flow. The van passes another barrier gate. A couple of older houses that narrowly escaped being demolished by lava flows will be pointed out near Yaiza. The minibus returns to the visitor centre, which is worth a few moments of study and is full of information, much of it in English.

The Ruta de Termesana is restricted to those who join a guided walk

WALK 42
Volcanic Coast Walk

Distance:	29km (18 miles)
Start:	Yaiza
Finish:	Mancha Blanca
Map:	1:50,000 Military Map Sheet 47-36
Terrain:	Easy road walking at the beginning and end, but a long, rough and rocky coastal path in the middle. On very windy days sea-spray washes over the coastal path.

This is the only walk permitted on an *anytime* basis in the Parque Nacional Timanfaya. You can request a guide from the national park visitor centre to show you along the route, but that has to be negotiated personally. This is a very long day's walk if you are using buses to Yaiza and away from Mancha Blanca as this includes lengthy road walks at the beginning and end. The middle part is rough, rocky and hard going across jagged and uneven coastal lava flows. If you can arrange to be dropped off and collected by car, then you can complete this stretch without the long road walks. Bear in mind that this coastline has only existed since the 1730s! Please see the map on p. 195.

Walk down the road from Yaiza to a complex roundabout outside the village, where the road for El Golfo runs underneath the main road. Follow the road across a broad dip full of black, jagged lava from which green and pink hills rise. When the road ascends gently, you can use a track on a parallel course, just to the right, to cross the gap between **Vieja Gabriela** and Pico Redondo. Follow the road downhill and there are good views to the right into the Parque Nacional Timanfaya. Just after the K4 marker, an unsignposted track heads off to the right. If you can arrange to be dropped here, then you can save covering the initial road-walk from Yaiza.

The track passes a few cultivated plots, then drops gently downhill with fine views of volcanic peaks, and jagged black lava all around. There are two tracks on the right that have chains across them, and access is forbidden except to local farmers and walkers being guided by national park staff, such as on Walk 41. Head straight onwards to follow the track between tall white pillars to approach the coast on the only line available to walkers in the national park. The track is red and cindery, descending a little, then rising past a couple of houses.

Keep left at a fork (in any case right is marked as private). The track descends onto a jagged lava flow and vehicles are forbidden further access. A Timanfaya devil has a 'no cars' sign skewered on its fork! Beyond is the isolated little peak of Montaña de Halcones, designated as the Monumento Natural del Islote de Halcones. In 1730 this was a coastal feature, so you can see by what extent the awesome lava flows added to the coastline of Lanzarote.

Follow the track past a barrier gate and walk down into a green hollow in front of the lava snout. The track moves back onto the lava and continues down towards the coast. Just before reaching a sign forbidding camping, follow a narrow, cindery track that cuts across the lava flow to the right. The stones are loose and uneven, so watch your feet. The path drifts to the coast, reaching a boiling cauldron where the sea pounds against a deep cleft in the cliffs. Local fishermen say the sea is angry after losing so much territory to the lava flow! Follow the winding coastal path, which is slow going as the path is vague in places and always rough and stony underfoot. In gales or storms the cliffs are lashed by spray and this walk would be inadvisable. There is little in the way of landmarks to help gauge progress, so simply keep walking. In most places the rock is quite bare, lacking even a crust of lichen.

There is a low stretch along the coast, where a bouldery, grey and gritty beach is covered in flotsam and jetsam with little clumps of uvilla growing in hollows. This is the **Caleta de la Ensenada**. Occasionally, colonies of gulls might be noticed far inland on the rough and jagged lava flows. The skyline is full of volcanic peaks and you may spot the tour buses negotiating the bendy **Ruta de los Volcanes**. Look ahead to spot a post and climb from the beach up onto a mass of ropy lava.

There is no real path on the bare rock, so the trodden route is intermittent and only reappears on the stonier stretches. Keep looking ahead to spot the continuation so avoiding wandering aimlessly through the rugged landscape. Pass a trig point at **Paletón**, where the sea pounds back and forth against the rocky clefts in the

Transport:
Arrecife Bus 6 links Yaiza with Playa Blanca, Puerto del Carmen and Arrecife. Bus 15 links Mancha Blanca with Arrecife. The walk can be effectively halved if you can be dropped off and collected by car.

Refreshments:
There are a few bar restaurants at Yaiza and a shop and a couple of bar restaurants at Mancha Blanca.

Montaña El Golfo can be seen as the track descends towards the coast

cliffs in a fury. The path continues, then finally turns round a little headland and drops onto a small grey beach. This is the **Playa de la Madera**. Walk up a track, enjoying the easier walking surface, and continue roughly parallel to the coast. Follow the track inland, unless you can arrange to be collected at this point.

A scrubby slope gives way to more black, jagged lava. Looking to either side reveals little islands, or *islotes* of greenery that represent the hills on the old land surface before the lava rolled over the low-lying parts in between. The track crosses a large area of scrub, then runs up through another more extensive lava flow. Wide-open views enable you to track these flows back towards their source in the **Montañas del Fuego**. Take particular note of how the lava spilled around Caldera Blanca, which can be studied at closer quarters on Walk 43.

Most of the time only hills are seen while looking ahead but later a solitary white building catches the eye on the skyline. The track runs up to a road, that in turn climbs to a road junction where the white building is situated. Keep straight on if you want to end at Tinajo, or turn right to reach Mancha Blanca in slightly less time. Higgledy-piggledy stone-walled fields are full of black cinders, which have the peculiar property of keeping the soil beneath moist in any weather. Indeed, the cinders will actually absorb minute amounts of water from the humid night air and transmit it down into the soil. This is why you see so many cinder quarries around Lanzarote and on the some of the other Canary Islands. The road reaches a junction where you turn right, then left to approach **Mancha Blanca**. The Snack Bar Mancha Blanca and a small shop are passed, then further up the road, near the sports pitch, is the Centro Socio Cultural Mancha Blanca and the Bodega la Montañeta. The bus stop is nearby, so you could eat and drink while watching for the bus.

WALK 43
Caldera Blanca

Distance:	21km (13 miles)
Start/Finish:	Mancha Blanca
Maps:	1:50,000 Military Map Sheets 47-36 and 48-36
Terrain:	Mostly low-level along often rough and rocky ground, with one hill climb. However, paths, tracks and roads are used throughout.

Transport:
Arrecife Bus 15 serves Mancha Blanca from Arrecife

Refreshments:
There is a shop and a couple of bar restaurants in Mancha Blanca.

Start near the sports pitch at **Mancha Blanca** at around 300m (1000ft). The Centro Socio Cultural Mancha Blanca and the Bodega la Montañeta stand at a road junction. Follow the road downhill as signposted for Yaiza, passing a small shop and the Snack Bar Mancha Blanca. The road leaves the village on a raised embankment and bends left at a junction with another road and a track. Follow the track straight onwards, passing fields of black cinders bounded by higgledy-piggledy drystone walls. There is a turning space where the cinder

The Caldera Blanca is a remarkable volcanic crater and the crowning glory of the Parque Natural de los Volcanes. The circumference of the crater is 3.5km (2¼ miles). The floor of the crater lies at 143m (469ft), while the highest point on the rim is 458m (1503ft). The land level outside the crater slopes from about 270m to 150m (885ft to 490ft). The volcano has long been dormant, but the lava flows surrounding it spilled from the nearby Montañas del Fuego and date from the 1730s.

track is blocked to traffic, and at that point a path continues just to the right. This path is stony underfoot and crosses a jagged, bouldery lava flow. There is a dip into a valley where the rock is more thickly crusted with lichen. After meandering further across the lava flow the path reaches the *islote* called **Montaña Caldereta** and drops down to the right. There is quite a difference between the dark, rugged lava flow and the smooth and vegetated slopes of this little volcano. As the path turns round the lower slopes you can peep into the crater, but beyond lies the much larger Caldera Blanca.

Follow the path uphill a short way on the slopes of Montaña Caldereta, but watch carefully to spot the path crossing the rugged lava flow to the right. When the path reaches the lower slopes of **Caldera Blanca**, walk downhill a little, then follow a narrow path that slices diagonally up the steep slope. It quickly reaches a low point on the rim of an immense crater, where you can gaze in awe at the level floor and gullied walls. Now turn your attention to the summit. Turn left and follow the rounded rim uphill. The ground is often rocky, but the gradient is fairly easy, and the summit is marked by a prominent trig point at 458m (1503ft). This is an excellent viewpoint, providing an overview of this day's walk and taking in the Montañas del Fuego in the Parque Nacional Timanfaya, with the vast expanse of jagged lava flows smothering most of the landscape. The southern parts of Lanzarote give way to a small portion of Fuerteventura. There are plenty of other hills in view, almost all of them are old volcanoes. Far to the north-east are the minor Canary Islands of Graciosa, Montaña Clara and Alegranza.

Continue walking round the crater rim to descend. The western side is steeper and rockier and leads down to a broad gap. If you want to drop down into the crater bottom use a zigzag path on the right. Otherwise look carefully down the rugged slope to the left and follow another zigzag path down towards a track on the lower slopes, next to some low hills. Turn left to follow the track down past cultivated plots, passing a couple of buildings. When a junction is reached, and the main track swings right, walk straight on across a lava flow to reach another track junction where you turn left. Follow the track gradually uphill. There are patches of scrub and little *islotes* can be seen, but later the lava flows bear little vegetation and are simply crusted with lichen. Caldera Blanca is now to the left and its aspect has changed so that it looks like three rounded hills. The track approaches a Parque Nacional sign and runs close to the shattered volcano of Caldera Roja. As the track rises closer to this little volcano, there is another Parque Nacional sign, with a Timanfaya devil skewering a walker on its toasting fork! Casual walking is simply not permitted in the national park, so this is as close as you can get. The track passes a slope of fine cinders and runs across a hollow in the hills that is full of rough and spiky lava flows. You will reach a road that is used by vehicles to access the national park.

If you want to go to the national park as an extension to this walk, turn right and right again. You will have to pay at the entrance but will only be able to walk up to a restaurant and souvenir shop on the **Islote del Hilario**. The standard tour involves being given a handful of freshly dug gravel to handle, which is hot even when dug from a single spade-depth. You can watch a man push some scrub into a hole in the ground, where it bursts into flames. Another man pours water into pipes sunk into the ground, where it spurts back as a jet of steam. If you are bursting for a pee, please play safe and use the toilets! There is no further access to the national park on foot and the only way to explore it further, apart from Walks 41 and 42, is to join a coach tour along the **Ruta de los Volcanes** and view the landscape through the windows while listening to a taped commentary.

If you reach the road and don't wish to visit the national park, then simply turn left to return to Mancha Blanca. The road runs across an extensive area of

Caldera Blanca is an island, or *islote* of greenery in this barren rocky terrain. Walking across the lava flows would be difficult, but there are good paths and tracks allowing Caldera Blanca and the surrounding area to be explored. The national park is approached closely and the park visitor centre is included towards the end of this route. Please see the map on p. 195.

The rocky crater rim of Caldera Blanca is easy to follow and offers fine views

blocky lava, before the little cinder cone of **Montaña Tingata** rises to the left. There is a path and track allowing a walk around its base, giving a break from the road and offering a fine view back to Caldera Blanca. Keep following the road to find the national park visitor centre, or Centro de Visitantes e Interpretación de Mancha Blanca, off to the left. There are plenty of informative displays with English commentaries here, as well as an audio-visual show. This is also where you make enquiries if you want to join the guided walk as described in Walk 41. After exploring the visitor centre, simply follow the road straight back to **Mancha Blanca** for food, drink and the bus.

WALK 44

Mancha Blanca to Monumento al Campesino

Distance:	18km (11 miles)
Start:	Mancha Blanca
Finish:	Monumento al Campesino
Map:	1:50,000 Military Map Sheet 48-36
Terrain:	Mostly low-level across rugged lava flows. A series of roads, tracks and rough stony paths are used.

Transport:
Arrecife Bus 15 links Arrecife with Mancha Blanca and the Monumento al Campesino. Midweek services 15, 16, 17 and 18 also link the Monumento al Campesino with Arrecife.

Refreshments:
There is a small shop and a couple of bar restaurants at Mancha Blanca. The Monumento al Campesino has a large restaurant.

Follow the road south from **Mancha Blanca**. There are a couple of fields either side of the road, followed by a few houses, then the road crosses a low gap between two little hills. The scene ahead is of extensive blocky lava flows surrounded by hills. Turn right along a tarmac road on this gap and almost immediately take a broad dirt road to the left. The slopes of Montaña del Cortijo rise to the right, while lava flows stretch away to the left. The track leads to some cultivated plots, then swings left across the barren lava flow to reach the foot of **Montaña Los Rodeos**. Keep right and follow the main track round the hillside, avoiding any tracks climbing up the steep slope. The cinder slopes are gradually being quarried away, but far to the right are views of the protected peaks of the Parque Nacional Timanfaya. There is a fork in the track and a gentle ascent to the left leads to a broad crest, offering better views of the Montañas del Fuego.

You could walk further along the crest to enjoy views from the far end, but that means retracing your steps later. To continue the walk simply swing to the left at the point where you reached the crest and descend. A track is reached at the foot of the slope and

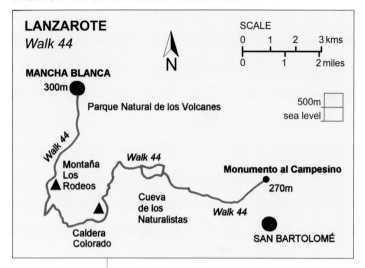

by turning left it can be followed between the hillside and a very rough and blocky lava flow. Walk gently uphill and watch carefully for a rugged track heading off onto the lava flow to the right. Follow the track and try and keep to the clearest line, though there are intersections with other vague tracks and much of the surface of the lava flow has been stripped and removed. Some walkers might find it difficult to distinguish between the natural surface of the lava and the quarried surface as it is all rough and rocky underfoot! A couple of prominent, spiky craters are noticed rising above this rugged wasteland, then the track leads to a road.

Cross over the road and drift slightly to the left to crunch across stony ground to reach the lower slopes of the **Caldera Colorado**. Join a track and take a right turn around to the back of this old volcano. The Caldera Colorado has a strikingly red slope, while the lichen-encrusted rocks are pale green. This broad area of ancient lava is surrounded by hills and there are dune-like heaps of cinders dotted with huge boulders. The back of Caldera Colorado has been quarried. Follow the track until there is a clear junction with another track in an area supporting a few shrubs.

Turn right to follow another clear track across a quarried lava flow, with more dune-like heaps of cinders to the right. When a clear fork in the track is reached, keep right, and keep low around the vegetated cindery hillside. There are views across the lichen-crusted lava flow to the gap near Mancha Blanca where this walk started. Note the fig trees planted in the sheltered gully between the lava flow and the hillside. Follow the track round into a large amphitheatre and keep to the clearest course across the rugged terrain. Head towards a house on the skyline, with a solitary tall palm tree to the right. A walled track is reached and there is a choice of routes. Either follow the walled track past vines and a house to reach a road, or turn right alongside the wall and make a wider circuit to reach the road. The latter course is admittedly very rugged towards the end, but it offers the chance to see at least a small part of the huge collapsed lava tube called the **Cueva de los Naturalistas**.

If you want to take the easy course turn right along the road. If you decide upon the difficult course turn left along the road. A track with a chain across it leads to a house on the other side of the road. There is another track nearby that passes close to the house, but continues onto another broad area of lichen-crusted lava. This is smooth in places, often ropy, with waves and depressions where it has been squeezed as it solidified. It is riddled with tubes, some of which have collapsed. The whole area is attractively surrounded by hills. Follow the track off the lava towards some houses. Take a right and left turn and pass areas sprouting vines before the road becomes tarmac. Keep walking onwards to reach the main road and turn left. After all the time spent in the open you will welcome the nice shady spot to sit in by the road junction.

Keep following the main road, then either turn right to reach the village of **San Bartolomé** and the Museo Tanit, or keep left for the **Monumento al Campesino**.

The Parque Natural de los Volcanes that abuts the Parque Nacional Timanfaya doesn't have the same restrictions on walking. The landscape south of Mancha Blanca includes vast lava flows around 300m (1000ft), punctuated by old volcanoes rising as islands, or *islotes* above the general level. Hidden in the middle of this area is the Monumento Natural de la Cueva de los Naturalistas, which is a long lava tube that has collapsed along much of its length. The walk ends at the Monumento al Campesino, said to be at the exact centre of Lanzarote, celebrating the life and traditions of the peasantry. Please refer to the map on p. 210.

A detour includes views of the Monumento Natural Cueva de los Naturalistas

The tall white monument was created by the artist César Manrique, and represents a peasant farmer with his animals. Alongside are blindingly white buildings that incorporate traditional designs and artefacts from Lanzarote's agricultural past. There is a huge underground restaurant offering food and drink if you have a long time to wait for a bus.

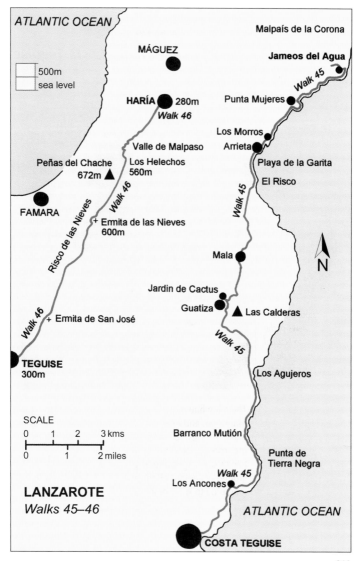

ATLANTIC OCEAN

Malpaís de la Corona

MÁGUEZ

Jameos del Agua

500m
sea level

Walk 45

HARÍA 280m
Walk 46

Punta Mujeres

Valle de Malpaso

Los Morros

Los Helechos
560m

Arrieta

Peñas del Chache
672m ▲

Playa de la Garita

El Risco

FAMARA

Risco de las Nieves

Walk 46

+ Ermita de las Nieves
600m

Walk 45

Mala

Jardin de Cactus

Walk 46

Guatiza

▲ Las Calderas

+ Ermita de San José

Walk 45

● TEGUISE
300m

Los Agujeros

SCALE
0   1   2   3 kms
|—|—|—|—|
0   1   2 miles

Barranco Mutión

Punta de
Tierra Negra

LANZAROTE
Walks 45–46

Walk 45
Los Ancones

N

ATLANTIC OCEAN

● **COSTA TEGUISE**

WALK 45
Jameos del Agua to Costa Teguise

Distance:	25km (15½ miles)
Start:	Jameos del Agua
Finish:	Los Zocos at Costa Teguise
Map:	1:50,000 Military Map Sheets 48-35 and 48-36
Terrain:	Mostly low-level coastal walking using rugged paths, tracks and roads

This is a long, mostly coastal, walk with the middle section stretching further inland. It can be split into two halves at the Jardin de Cactus at Guatiza, where there are over two thousand specimens imaginatively arranged around a rocky hollow. The start of the walk is close to the caves of Jameos del Agua and the Cueva de los Verdes; both are part of an enormous lava tube stretching from Monte Corona, through the malpaís, to end beneath the sea. Visiting both places takes half a day and leaves no time to for the walk, so explore them at leisure some other time. The route ends at the bustling resort of Costa Teguise, but bus services allow it to be broken at a number of points. Map on p. 213.

The walk starts at a crossroads between the Cueva de los Verdes, which is uphill, and Jameos del Agua, which is downhill. These cave systems are part of a huge lava tube and are well worth exploring, but would take several hours from the day's walk. Follow the access road to Jameos del Agua, which was developed as an attraction by the artist César Manrique. Interestingly, it contains a deep pool of water full of blind crabs that are actually deep-sea crustaceans long thought to be extinct and known only from fossil records! Although essentially no more than a hole in the ground, Jameos del Agua includes a couple of bars, a swimming pool, exotic trees and flowers, an exhibition about vulcanism and a huge underground auditorium.

Just beyond the car park, a sign indicates there are toilets down to the left while a paved path leads down to the rocky shore. Turn right to follow a rough and stony coastal path to reach a trig point and a track. Follow the track onwards and it gives way to another rugged coastal path, with a drystone wall beneath the scrubby malpaís and the storm beach. Buildings are reached at Playa La Seba and you can pick your way around **Punta Mujeres** using narrow roads and little pathways. There are a couple of shops and bars just a short step inland. The main road is reached at a small development called Casitas del Mar, and there is an open space between it and **Los Morros**. Pass the Bar Restaurante El Lago at Los Morros, then a palm-fringed space and a stout stone pier before entering **Arrieta**. The houses are built close to the sea, so walk through the village by road. There are a couple of bar restaurants and shops on the way through. A foot-bridge leads across to the **Playa La Garita**, and you can walk either on the beach or just above it. At the end of the cobbly beach a low cliff path can be followed and there are views back to Jameos del Agua. When a couple of houses are seen ahead, cut inland a short way and walk alongside the main road.

There is a track running parallel to the main road. It later drifts away to the left of the road and runs past stone-walled fields. The track becomes a tarmac road and is followed straight through a crossroads. Turn right at the next junction, then go straight through the next, staggered, junction beside a transformer tower. Note the prickly pears, vines and tomatoes that grow alongside the track. A right turn leads back to the main road, where a left turn leads onto a long plaza in the middle of **Mala** which is shaded by palms and bougainvillea. There is a shop on the main road, as well as a couple of bar restaurants up to the left at the top end of the village.

Take the very last turn on the left on leaving the village to discover a road leading only to a house. A track continues onwards, bending to the right to run parallel to the main road, but at some distance from it. It rises through prickly pear plantations and offers fine views of the surrounding hills. At the top of the track, turn right along a road, noting a windmill ahead. Keep right to reach the **Jardin de Cactus**, which is well worth a visit.

The garden is couched in a rocky hollow where terraces are planted with a bewildering array of cacti. Wander up and down steps to see them all, and take the time to climb up to the windmill too. Hazards include walking off unprotected terraces and walking into spiky specimens! There is a bar restaurant and a souvenir shop selling live cactus plants if you want to

Transport:
Arrecife Bus 9 serves Guatiza, Mala, Arrieta, Punta Mujeres and Jameos del Agua from Arrecife and Orzola. Arrecife Bus 7 also serves Guatiza, Mala and Arrieta and Punta Mujeres from Arrecife and Maguez. Frequent Arrecife Bus 1 services link Costa Teguise and Arrecife

Refreshments:
There is a bar at Jameos del Agua, shops, bars and restaurants at Punta Mujeres, Los Morros, Arrieta and Mala, a restaurant at the Jardin de Cactus at Guatiza and plenty of shops, bars and restaurants at Costa Teguise.

Jameos del Agua is a lava tube crammed to the brim with interesting features

start your own garden back home. If your whole day grinds to a halt here, then it is time well spent. Again, this garden is essentially a hole in the ground, but it was developed into an imaginative attraction by the artist César Manrique. Sometimes, outside the garden, an old man might show you how the prickly pears are infested by the cochineal insect, which is harvested for its rich, red juice using a metal ladle to scrape them from the plant.

Leave the garden, avoiding the main road, and walk towards the foot of the hill called **Las Calderas**. Swing right by the road and aim to follow only the roads running closest to the hill, avoiding dead-ends that rise to the left. Pass the football pitch, identified by its floodlights, and reach a junction with another road. Turn left to follow the road away from **Guatiza**, down towards the coast. Do not walk all the way to the coast, but only until the houses and *salinas* (or salt-pans) at **Los Agujeros** can be seen to the left. When a prominent left turn is reached on the road, walk straight on along a broad dirt road. This crosses a level scrubland and serves a couple of houses along the coast. When you reach the rocky shore follow the track along it with a very tall drystone wall to your right. The track finally expires along the coast and one spur heads inland, but do not follow it.

Continue across the shallow and rocky Barranco Mutión, which has a small pool near its mouth. Follow a narrow, stony path, gradually gaining height. Enjoy the fine views both ways along the black cliffs. Turn around the rugged **Punta de Tierra Negra** in an area full of stony little hills. There is a trig point on one of them at only 51m (167ft). The land ahead is criss-crossed with paths and tracks. It is best to head straight for the huddle of houses at **Los Ancones** and follow a clear dirt road away from

There are over two thousand specimens to see around the Jardin de Cactus

them. This is quite dusty and if there are vehicles kicking up too much dust, you may prefer to walk near the coast. The dirt road leads to a junction with a main road, where a left turn leads round a bend and into the resort of **Costa Teguise**. Pass the Lanzarote Beach Club (or LBC) and look out for a short road on the left giving access to the busy Playa de los Charcos. Note the preserved windpumps that were once associated with *salinas* in this area. Buses turn around in the car park near the beach, but passengers are not allowed on board. Further along the main road, on the right, is Los Zocos Club Resort and the bus stop for Arrecife. Services are frequent, but if you want to stay for a while then there are plenty of places offering food and drink.

WALK 46
Teguise to Haría

The roads between Teguise and Haría are anything but direct, and bus services travel between those two places by a most peculiar route. However, in the past there was a direct line from one to the other, and this can still be followed today. Old tracks and paths can be linked over the highest parts of Lanzarote, passing the Ermita de las Nieves, running close to the summit of Peñas del Chache, and finally descending to the Valley of a Thousand Palms at Haría (as shown on the map, p. 213). It is a fairly easy walk that should leave plenty of time to explore both places, which have plenty of quaint corners and features of interest.

Distance:	13km (8 miles)
Start:	Teguise
Finish:	Haría
Maps:	1:50,000 Military Map Sheets 48-35 and 48-36
Terrain:	Hilly, but slopes are mostly fairly gentle. The route follows roads, tracks and paths and there is only one steep and rugged descent.

Teguise is a wonderful old town which served as the capital of Lanzarote until the middle of the 19th century. It is overlooked by the 16th century Castillo de Santa Bárbara, perched on a hill called Guanapay, just to the east of town. At the top end of town, around 300m (1000ft), is the Museum of Sacred Art, housed in a former church. To leave Teguise, follow cobbled streets towards the prominent tower of the Parish Church, dedicated to Nuestra Señora de Guadalupe, and founded in the 16th century. Walk across a large paved plaza from one arched entrance to another, then climb up a few steps onto a road. Go uphill a little and take a narrow road off to the left. Follow it to a sports stadium, then continue past it before turning left. A broad dirt road finally leaves Teguise.

Keep left at a fork in the dirt road and then, at the next fork, keep right to follow a clear track across a broad, shallow valley. A ruin stands to the right, and this was once the **Ermita de San José**. A cross-tracks lies beyond, and you simply walk straight through and follow a patchy track that slants uphill to the left on a scrubby slope. The ground is often stony and rocky, but the gradient is easy, and although the track virtually disappears towards the top, there is a broad dirt road high on the crest. Turn left to follow it uphill at a gentle gradient. At one point there is a view to the left over a steep edge that reveals the coastal village of La Caleta. Follow the road up past a building surrounded by squat antennae to reach the **Ermita de las Nieves**. This hilltop church is at an altitude of almost 600m (1970ft) and is surrounded by palms and flowers and has a big cindery car park. There are fine views southwards through Lanzarote to distant Fuerteventura, but looking ahead only the broad rise of **Peñas del Chache** is seen, with a military installation on top. There is no access to the summit, which is the highest point on Lanzarote at 672m (2205ft).

Keep left of the *ermita,* avoiding the road, to enjoy a brief view over the Risco de las Nieves to the coastal village of **Famara**. A clear track climbs gently towards **Peñas del Chache**, passing little white huts and black cinder fields. Cultivation almost reaches the top of the hill, but ends at the fence surrounding the military installation. A road is joined and this leads gently downhill to a junction. This is signposted back for the Mirador Riscos de Famara. Turn left down the main road to reach the Bar Restaurante Los Helechos, which also serves as a fine viewpoint overlooking the northern valleys and hills of Lanzarote from 560m (1840ft).

The main road descends in convoluted zigzags down the steep and rugged slopes of the **Valle de Malpaso**. There is no need for walkers to negotiate all these turns; simply look for gaps in the roadside barrier to discover a path heading more directly downhill. The path occasionally zigzags and in places the stone paving is uneven. It drops from a high part of the road, crosses the road and drops again, then crosses the road at a sign reading 'Valle de Malpaso'. A longer stretch of path cuts down across the slope and crosses the road a final time before becoming a clear track. There are so many palm trees that this area is known as the Valley of a Thousand Palms. Apparently, villagers were in the habit of celebrating the birth of each of their children

Transport:
Arrecife Bus 7 links Arrecife with Teguise and Haría. Arrecife Bus 9 and 10 also serve Teguise from Arrecife. Direct Sunday bus services 11, 12 and 13 serve Teguise from Costa Teguise, Puerto del Carmen and Playa Blanca respectively.

Refreshments:
There are shops, bars and restaurants at Teguise, and a bar restaurant above the Valle de Malpaso. Haría has a shop and a couple of bar restaurants.

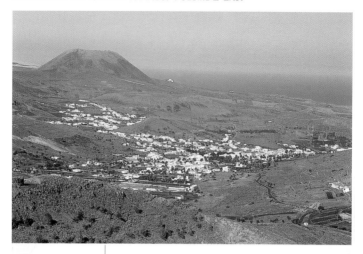

A fine view of Haría and Maguez from the Bar Restaurante Los Helechos

by burying the placenta and planting a palm on top. The practice ended some time ago, otherwise there would be nothing but palm trees in the valley!

A narrow road called the Calle Elvira Sanchez continues into the village of **Haría**. Continue down it even when the road is marked as no entry. The Calle el Puente naturally leads across a bridge at the bottom, and a right turn leads into a pleasant little plaza in the middle of the village at 280m (920ft). The Snack Bar Cafeteria Ney-Ya and Supermercado La Plaza are located here, and there are a couple of other places offering food and drink in the village. To find the bus stop, go behind the Supermercado and walk along another tree-lined plaza to reach a road behind the church.

ATLANTIC OCEAN

Montaña Bermeja

Playa Lambra

Walk 50

Reserva Marina
Isla e islotes del Graciosa

GRACIOSA

Walk 50

Pedro Barba

Caleta de Pedro Barba

Caleta del Burro

Parque Natural del
Archipélago Chinijo

Walk 49

Walk 50

Montaña
del Mojón

Caleta de Sebo

174m

Walk 49

ORZOLA

Montaña
Amarilla

La Punta
Salinas del Río

Mirador del Río

485m

Walk 47

SCALE

0   1   2   3 kms

0   1   2 miles

Walk 48

370m

Ye

ATLANTIC OCEAN

Monte Corona

Guatifay

Malpaís de la Corona

Pinnacle

Walk 47

Walk 47

N

520m

Walk 48

MÁGUEZ
260m

HARÍA

Riscos de Famara

Walk 48

500m

sea level

LANZAROTE
Walks 47–50

FAMARA

WALK 47
Máguez and Ye

The northern part of Lanzarote features a couple of quiet little villages, plenty of little farms, and in addition to the roads that run through the area there is a good network of paths and tracks. Buses serve Máguez and a fine circular walk can be enjoyed from this point. The route is actually in the form of a series of loops, so if time starts running short at any point, it is easy enough to take a short-cut by continueing along the road. The route wanders around the volcano of Monte Corona, touches the *malpaís* badlands below, climbs to the straggly village of Ye, and includes a couple of viewpoints overlooking the Riscos de Famara (as shown on the map on p. 221).

Distance:	20km (12½ miles)
Start/Finish:	Máguez
Map:	1:50,000 Military Map Sheet 48–35
Terrain:	Hilly, with several ascents and descents, but accomplished on a series of good roads, tracks and paths.

The bus to **Máguez** stops on a tiny plaza in the middle of the village at 260m (855ft). Turn right, as the bus does when it turns around, and follow the level road past the church. A crossroads is reached where there is a mirror on a pole advertising Malibu Tropical Coconut. Turn left and walk uphill by road. At the top this is the Calle las Casillas and a clear, walled track, fringed with palms, forks to the right. Follow this track away from Máguez, descending and climbing gently, with **Monte Corona** rising steeply to the left. Pass a water storage building, then note a big concrete apron for collecting rainwater on the steep hillside, around 370m (1215ft). The track descends across the cindery slope, through a landscape covered in higgledy-piggledy drystone walls. Keep left at a fork to join a road, then keep left again to walk straight uphill. A startling, white, fortress-like building stands on the slopes of Monte Corona called the Torrecilla de Domingo. There is also a view of the jagged crater on top of Monte Corona.

The road passes a couple of gate piers, then bends left and heads directly for the village called Ye. However, exit to the right on the road bend, down a clear track, and uphill a little to reach a junction with another track. Turn right downhill, noting the intricate patterns of the drystone walls around straggly vines. There are a few houses on the slope, then a road is reached around 180m (590ft). Turn left to pass below an interesting house and garden, then turn left again up another clear track. This one meanders uphill round the right-hand side of a jagged crater, overlooking a deep little valley, then passing a house and crossing over into a gentler high valley at Vega Grande. The tracks twists and turns past terraces and plots, gradually climbing towards **Ye**. When a road is joined, at around 370m (1215ft), you could turn right and head for the Mirador del Río, or simply head for the Restaurante el Volcán across the road. Following the road straight through the straggly village leads past the Centro Socio Cultural El Tefio Ye. There is a bus stop alongside though buses to Ye are not timetabled.

Follow the road out of the village, then turn sharp right along another road that leads to the Mirador del Río. Follow this road only down into a gentle hollow where there are a couple of houses, then turn left along a stone-paved track to reach a small car park. A stone-paved path and a few stone steps lead down to a viewpoint beside a pylon. Take a peep over the edge, where a path descends to the shore and is followed on Walk 48. For the time being, simply admire the view out to Graciosa, Montaña Clara and Alegranza. The Salinas del Rio are also in view at the foot of the cliff, close to the sea. Look carefully to the left of the viewpoint to spot a rocky cliff path, then follow this uphill and pass in front of a shuttered building. Climb further uphill and the rugged path drifts gradually inland onto an eroded slope. Follow a track inland, avoiding turnings and nearby houses, to descend past heaps of cinders to reach a junction with the main road. A big stone here indicates that the track is the **Camino de Guatifay**.

Turn right down the road and right again as signposted for the Guinate Tropical Park. Only a short way up the road, turn left up a prominent hill track. This climbs steadily past slopes of flowery scrub and cultivation plots, with increasing views over Graciosa and northern Lanzarote. Keep climbing towards a little house

Transport:
Arrecife Bus 7 serves Máguez from Arrecife

Refreshments:
There are a couple of bars and restaurants at Máguez and Ye.

A track climbs gradually uphill towards Monte Corona and the village of Ye

at the top of the valley, passing a junction of tracks and heading for the edge of the rugged cliffs of the Riscos de Famara around 520m (1705ft). Look over the edge and you can see a precarious path that is used on Walk 48. The track swings gradually to the left, heading inland, and passes the boundary fence of an aircraft beacon on a gentle hilltop.

Follow the access road downhill from the beacon, but short-cut down a cindery slope when the road begins to zigzag. Continue down the road towards some farm buildings, then just before reaching them, cut off down a stony track to the right. This becomes a narrow path on a scrubby slope and leads down to the road beside some buildings at the top end of **Máguez**. Walk down the Calle la Caldera and continue down the Calle San Francisco to reach the centre of the village. When the little plaza and shelter are reached at a crossroads, either wait there for a bus, or walk a few more paces for refreshment at the cafeteria bar attached to the Centro Democratico de Máguez.

WALK 48
Mirador del Río to Famara

Distance:	23km (14¼ miles)
Start:	Mirador del Río
Finish:	Famara
Map:	1:50,000 Military Map Sheet 48–35
Terrain:	Rugged cliff paths with a danger of rockfall and landslip in places

The **Mirador del Río**, at 485m (1590ft), was imaginatively developed from an old coastal lookout by the artist César Manrique. You have to pay to enter and enjoy the best views, but there is also a bar and toilets as well as welcome shelter from the sun or wind. The small islands of Graciosa, Montaña Clara and Alegranza can be seen, as can the Salinas del Río, which are the oddly coloured salt-pans at the foot of the cliff. These can be visited on this particular walk. To start the walk, leave the car park and take the road to the right along the top of the cliffs. There are reasonably good views over the edge before the road drifts inland into a rugged, cultivated hollow. Watch for a ruined building and a stone-paved track to the right that leads to a small car park. A stone-paved path and a few stone steps lead down to a viewpoint beside a pylon. Take a peep over the edge to study the path running downhill, and its continuation to the right towards the Salinas del Río.

Walk carefully down the path, which quickly becomes rough, stony and slippery underfoot. The flowery scrub on the steep slopes is interesting and contains some species that you won't find anywhere else. Before reaching the bottom of the slope there is an option to head off to the left, which shortens the

This is the best cliff walk on Lanzarote. However, be warned that it is rough and stony underfoot and there is a danger of rockfall and landslip. It has been hacked and blasted along the rugged cliff face of the Riscos de Famara, from Famara to the Salinas del Río and there is every chance that a landslip may one day close the route. There is a splendid viewpoint at the start, though you have to pay to use it. A steep descent leads down to the coast, followed by the long, rugged, crumbling cliff path that rises and falls along the length of the Riscos de Famara. It is recommended that you have a look at parts of this walk from viewpoints on Walks 45 and 46, before attempting to follow it. Map on p. 221.

Transport:
Use taxis to reach
the start and then to
leave at the end of
the walk

Refreshments:
The Mirador del Río
has a bar at the start
of the walk. The
Restaurante Famara
is at the end of the
walk.

route by omitting the Salinas del Río. For the full walk, keep right and also bear in mind that there are a couple of paths leading down to small sandy beaches. The path is broad and easy on the lower slopes and passes through a drystone wall on the way to the salinas. Either head straight for the *salinas* and the pillar on **La Punta**, or complete an anti-clockwise walk around the *salinas* instead. The pylon line descending the cliffs to reach the pillar on La Punta, continues along the sea bed to supply power to Caleta de Sebo over on Graciosa. Have a close look at the *salinas*, where sea water slowly evaporates to leave a crust of salt.

Retrace your steps southwards from the *salinas*, but instead of climbing back up the steep slope, follow the broad and easy path straight onwards. It rises across a spiky ancient lava flow, but most of the slopes are thick with scrub. Keep to the main path and avoid a path heading down to the shore. The path is a broad ledge at times, high above a scrubby slope and tucked into the base of a cliff. At a higher level it crosses crumbling gullies where care is needed. There is a danger

Looking down on the rugged cliff path is a good idea before following it

of rockfalls and landslips, so avoid this walk in wet or windy weather. The path begins to level out when a prominent **pinnacle** is reached beyond some eroded gullies, at around 200m (655ft). The path is narrow in places as it contours across the cliff. The small islands to the north of Lanzarote appear to pass from sight, only to reappear from time to time. Looking ahead, the twin coastal villages of Famara and La Caleta are seen, but trying to spot the line of the path across the cliff face is disheartening, as it always looks as though it has vanished completely! It gets better on the final descent, eventually passing a little house, then a track leads to a bigger house hidden among trees and shrubs.

Follow the track to a junction and turn right to walk almost down to the beach. Turn left along a track that runs through bouldery scrub, then continue across a sandy area or a higher cobble beach past the houses at **Famara**. The Restaurante Famara is available here, tucked away among the bungalows. The bus service is no use to walkers, so you will have to leave by taxi.

A bouldery sandy scrub leads the eye towards the Montaña Amarilla

GRACIOSA

Though Graciosa is really part of Lanzarote, it is a separate island and belongs to an archipelago of small islands to the north of Lanzarote. It is served by daily ferries from Orzola to Caleta de Sebo, and there are a couple of places offering accommodation. It is essentially a desert island, covered in sandy scrub, with a charm and aspect all of its own and distinct from the other seven Canary Islands. Two routes are offered, running north and west from Caleta de Sebo to make a tour all the way round Graciosa. Walkers should make the effort to visit Graciosa, and if possible, stay overnight and experience the solitude of the place when all the day visitors have departed. The small islands and the sea around them are protected as a marine nature reserve.

WALK 49
Caleta de Sebo and the West

Distance:	14km (8¾ miles)
Start/Finish:	Caleta de Sebo, Graciosa
Map:	1:50,000 Military Map sheet 48-35
Terrain:	Low-level sandy or stony coastal tracks, as well as a steep and rocky little hill climb

Transport:
Arrecife Bus 9 runs from Arrecife to Orzola then take the daily ferry service from Orzola to Caleta de Sebo on Graciosa

Refreshments:
There are a few bar restaurants at Orzola and Caleta de Sebo

Leave the ferry at **Caleta de Sebo** and keep to the left across a concrete square at the harbourside. Follow a broad, paved path onwards to a sandy beach, then head straight inland from the Restaurante Girasol. The sandy streets of Caleta de Sebo are left behind in no time and a broad dirt road runs away from the village, heading for a wide gap in the middle of the island. The landscape bears a thin covering of scrub and gentle sandy slopes merge into the steep hillside of **Montaña del Mojón**, to the left of the gap. The sand is often quite

This is a quiet circuit around the western parts of Graciosa. The route basically runs across the island from Caleta de Sebo, round the back of Montaña del Mojón and then alongside an increasingly rugged coast. The path is good, but it ends rather abruptly on the lower slopes of Montaña Amarilla. A vague path leads up onto this old volcano, which proves to be a splendid viewpoint, and a half-circuit can be made around the crumbling crater rim. Easy sandy tracks and beach walks lead back to Caleta de Sebo. See the map on p. 221 for further information. The walk can be accomplished between the first and last ferry.

firm underfoot as it is a calcareous shell sand rather than silica. Cross the gap and descend gently, keeping to the left at junctions with other tracks, hugging the lower slopes of Montaña del Mojón. The last left fork leads onto a stonier track that crosses a stony scrubland. Descend gently towards the coast with views of the neighbouring islands of Montaña Clara and Alegranza. You will pass an area of low walls surrounding old cultivation plots.

Here the rocky coast may be taking a pounding from the sea even if all was calm at Caleta de Sebo. A track leads inland, back across the island if needed, otherwise continue parallel to, though quite a way from, the rocky shore. The track is sandy and, as it leaves the broad bay of **Caleta del Burro**, there are beach cobbles alongside it. The track is indistinct in places as it moves further round the coast, crossing dark gravel and scrub. It ends abruptly on the lower slopes of **Montaña Amarilla**, overlooking a rocky bay where ochreous shades dominate and the Riscos de Famara rise steep and bold across in Lanzarote. Do not be tempted to pick a way round the rocky bay on the sloping ledge, as it is unsafe. Instead, climb up the steep and crumbling rocky ridge, following a rather vague path. Take care not to slip on gritty patches. The crater rim at the top has a much clearer path and views take in the small islands north of Lanzarote. The trig point is to the right, standing at only 174m (571ft).

Walk around the rocky crater rim to find a descending steep and stony path. Towards the bottom of the path, swing right and follow a gentler path down around the base of the hill, to reach the little beach at Playa de la Cocina. This is a popular nude bathing spot, while surfers make sport out in the bay. Follow a sandy jeep track away from the bay, looping uphill and inland. Keep to the right and you can head down to the shore and walk along the sandy beaches instead. Later, a shallow saltwater lagoon appears at the Bahía del Salado. If the tide allows, you can pass between the lagoon and the sea, and notice how a rocky ledge is responsible for

holding the water in place. Otherwise the vehicle track you are following runs on the landward side of the lagoon. All that remains is to walk along either the track or the beach, both of which are as sandy as each other, to return to **Caleta de Sebo**. Most ferry passengers enjoy food and drink at the Restaurante Cafeteria El Varadero facing the harbour, allowing them to board the ferry at the last minute.

The Playa de la Cocina is a small beach at the foot of Montaña Amarilla

WALK 50
Caleta de Sebo and the North

Distance:	18km (11 miles)
Start/Finish:	Caleta de Sebo, Graciosa
Maps:	1:50,000 Military Map Sheets 48-34 and 48-35
Terrain:	Low-level sandy or stony coastal tracks, which are mostly clear underfoot.

231

This is a popular day's walk, making a circuit all the way round the northern half of Graciosa. Keep an eye on the time if hoping to complete the walk between ferries, and judge whether you can spare the time to visit the little village of Caleta de Pedro Barba. The tracks are mostly clear and obvious, and the whole circuit is used by cyclists, so you can follow their wheel marks most of the time (please see the map on p. 221). This walk takes you as close as you can get to the smallest of the Canary Islands, which sprawl northwards from Graciosa. They are all protected as part of the Parque Natural del Archipélago Chinijo and the Reserva Marina Isla e islotes del Graciosa.

Leave the ferry at **Caleta de Sebo** and keep to the left across a concrete square at the harbourside. Follow a broad, paved path onwards to a sandy beach, then head straight inland from the Restaurante Girasol. The sandy streets of Caleta de Sebo are left behind in no time and a broad dirt road runs away from the village, heading for a wide gap in the middle of the island. The landscape bears a thin covering of scrub and gentle, sandy slopes merge into the steep hillside of **Pedro Barba**, the oddly patterned hill to the right of the gap. The sand is often quite firm underfoot as it is a calcareous shell sand rather than silica. Cross the gap and descend gently, keeping to the right at a fork before the track splits four ways. The left leads back onto the main dirt road, the next right to cinder quarries on the hillside, while the next right is the one you should follow across the hillside (the last one leads only to nearby cultivated plots). Rise gently across the slope, enjoying views back to the Riscos de Famara at the northern end of Lanzarote. The stony track later descends into a stony, scrubby hollow and there are no habitations in sight. When a triangular junction is reached, however, a little huddle of houses can be seen to the right. This is **Caleta de Pedro Barba** and is worth a quick visit.

Follow the track and keep to the left of the houses, passing a boat on a cinder heap that is studded with cacti. This is a reminder of the little village's former fishing industry. Keep left of a solar power station and walk round to the harbour. The dumpy little houses are very attractive and are surrounded by palms and cacti. Complete a circuit round the village, then walk back along the access track to return to the triangular junction. Follow the track further into an empty wilderness, from stony and sandy scrub onto hard calcareous sand, studded with millions of tiny shells. Twin hills appear ahead. The reddish Montaña Bermeja is on Graciosa, but Montaña Clara is a separate island, and Alegranza is seen more distantly. The track seems to head for Alegranza as it drifts gently down towards the shore. Keep left to pass round a sandy bay at **Playa Lambra**.

Just beyond the bay the track crosses stone-studded ground and suddenly turns left inland. Avoid the lesser track to the right, which is a dead-end. The main track climbs very gently up a slope of stony, sandy scrub, passing over a very broad gap between **Montaña Bermeja** and Pedro Barba. There is only a small cultivated area off to the left, and the track runs straight ahead and includes views of Peñas del Chache, which is the highest point on Lanzarote, and the Montañas del Fuego in the Parque Nacional Timanfaya.

As you descend to a junction the track becomes cindery. If there is time to spare turn right to walk down to a little beach with a grand view of Montaña Clara, otherwise turn left to return to Caleta de Sebo. The track runs level, then rises on a stony slope and passes a dump. Looking back reveals good views of the small islands, while ahead there are a couple of cultivated plots. After crossing the broad rise the track descends through the broad gap in the middle of Graciosa, between Pedro Barba and Montaña del Mojón. When a junction is reached in the middle of the gap, keep right to walk back along the broad dirt road that was used earlier in the day. The Riscos de Famara on Lazarote look bold and dramatic on the descent. There is a track branching to the left that is worth following down to **Caleta de Sebo**. It leads to a little plaza and the island church, from where you can pick a way along the narrow, sandy streets to return to the harbour. Most ferry passengers enjoy food and drink at the Restaurante Cafeteria El Varadero facing the harbour, which allows them to board the ferry at the last minute.

Transport:
Arrecife Bus 9 runs from Arrecife to Orzola then take the daily ferry service from Orzola to Caleta de Sebo on Graciosa

Refreshments:
There are a few bar restaurants at Orzola and Caleta de Sebo.

APPENDIX: TOPOGRAPHICAL GLOSSARY

Apart from a few placenames which are derived from original Guanche words, most names on the maps are Spanish. Several words crop up time and again and are usually very descriptive of particular types of landforms, colours and sizes. The following list of common words helps to identify what some of the places on maps or signposts mean.

Agua	water
Alto/alta	high
Arenas	sands
Arroyo	stream
Asomada	promontory
Bajo/baja	low
Barranco	ravine
Barranquillo	small ravine
Blanco/blanca	white
Boca	gap
Cabeza	head
Caldera	crater
Calle	street
Camino	path/track
Cañada	gully
Canal	watercourse
Carretera	road
Casa	house
Casa forestal	forestry house
Collada/degollada	col/gap/saddle
Colorada	coloured
Corral	farmyard/corral
Cruz	cross/crossroads
Cuevas	caves
Cumbre	ridge/crest
De/del	of the
El/la/los/las	the
Embalse	reservoir

Era	threshing floor
Ermita	chapel/shrine
Estacion de guaguas	bus station
Fuente	fountain/spring
Galeria	water gallery
Gordo	fat/giant
Grande	big
Guagua	bus
Hoya	valley
Ladera	slope
Llano	plain
Lomo	spur/ridge
Montaña	mountain
Morro	nose
Negro/negra	black
Nieve	snow
Nuevo/nueva	new
Paso	pass
Pequeno	small
Pico	peak
Piedra	rock
Pino/pinar	pine
Playa	beach
Plaza	town square
Puerto	port/pass
Punta	point
Risco	cliff
Roja	red
Roque	rock
San/santa	saint
Sendero	route/path
Valle	valley
Verde	green
Vieja/viejo	old
Volcán	volcano

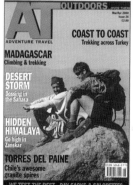

LISTING OF CICERONE GUIDES

NORTHERN ENGLAND LONG DISTANCE TRAILS
- THE DALES WAY
- THE ISLE OF MAN COASTAL PATH
- THE PENNINE WAY
- THE ALTERNATIVE COAST TO COAST
- NORTHERN COAST-TO-COAST
- THE RELATIVE HILLS OF BRITAIN
- MOUNTAINS ENGLAND & WALES
  VOL 1 WALES
  VOL 2 ENGLAND

CYCLING
- BORDER COUNTRY BIKE ROUTES
- THE CHESHIRE CYCLE WAY
- THE CUMBRIA CYCLE WAY
- THE DANUBE CYCLE WAY
- LANDS END TO JOHN O'GROATS CYCLE GUIDE
- ON THE RUFFSTUFF –
  84 BIKE RIDES IN NORTH ENGLAND
- RURAL RIDES NO.1 WEST SURREY
- RURAL RIDES NO.1 EAST SURREY
- SOUTH LAKELAND CYCLE RIDES
- THE WAY OF ST JAMES
  LE PUY TO SANTIAGO – CYCLIST'S
- CYCLE TOURING IN SPAIN
- THE LOIRE CYCLE ROUTE

LAKE DISTRICT AND MORECAMBE BAY
- CONISTON COPPER MINES
- CUMBRIA WAY & ALLERDALE RAMBLE
- THE CHRONICLES OF MILNTHORPE
- THE EDEN WAY
- FROM FELL AND FIELD
- KENDAL – A SOCIAL HISTORY
- A LAKE DISTRICT ANGLER'S GUIDE
- LAKELAND TOWNS
- LAKELAND VILLAGES
- LAKELAND PANORAMAS
- THE LOST RESORT?
- SCRAMBLES IN THE LAKE DISTRICT
- MORE SCRAMBLES IN THE LAKE DISTRICT
- SHORT WALKS IN LAKELAND
  BOOK 1: SOUTH
  BOOK 2: NORTH
  BOOK 3: WEST
- ROCKY RAMBLER'S WILD WALKS
- RAIN OR SHINE
- ROADS AND TRACKS OF THE LAKE DISTRICT
- THE TARNS OF LAKELAND
  VOL 1: WEST
- THE TARNS OF LAKELAND VOL 2: EAST
- WALKING ROUND THE LAKES
- WALKS SILVERDALE/ARNSIDE
- WINTER CLIMBS IN LAKE DISTRICT

NORTH-WEST ENGLAND
- WALKING IN CHESHIRE
- FAMILY WALKS IN FOREST OF BOWLAND
- WALKING IN THE FOREST OF BOWLAND
- LANCASTER CANAL WALKS
- WALKER'S GUIDE TO LANCASTER CANAL
- CANAL WALKS VOL 1: NORTH
- WALKS FROM THE LEEDS-LIVERPOOL CANAL
- THE RIBBLE WAY
- WALKS IN RIBBLE COUNTRY
- WALKING IN LANCASHIRE
- WALKS ON THE WEST PENNINE MOORS
- WALKS IN LANCASHIRE WITCH COUNTRY
- HADRIAN'S WALL
  VOL 1 : THE WALL WALK
  VOL 2 : WALL COUNTRY WALKS

NORTH-EAST ENGLAND
- NORTH YORKS MOORS
- THE REIVER'S WAY
- THE TEESDALE WAY
- WALKING IN COUNTY DURHAM
- WALKING IN THE NORTH PENNINES
- WALKING IN NORTHUMBERLAND
- WALKING IN THE WOLDS
- WALKS IN THE NORTH YORK MOORS BOOKS 1 AND 2
- WALKS IN THE YORKSHIRE DALES BOOKS 1,2 AND 3
- WALKS IN DALES COUNTRY
- WATERFALL WALKS – TEESDALE & HIGH PENNINES
- THE YORKSHIRE DALES
- YORKSHIRE DALES ANGLER'S GUIDE

THE PEAK DISTRICT
- STAR FAMILY WALKS PEAK DISTRICT/STH YORKS
- HIGH PEAK WALKS
- WEEKEND WALKS IN THE PEAK DISTRICT
- WHITE PEAK WALKS
  VOL.1 NORTHERN DALES
  VOL.2 SOUTHERN DALES
- WHITE PEAK WAY
- WALKING IN PEAKLAND
- WALKING IN SHERWOOD FOREST
- WALKING IN STAFFORDSHIRE
- THE VIKING WAY

WALES AND WELSH BORDERS
- ANGLESEY COAST WALKS
- ASCENT OF SNOWDON
- THE BRECON BEACONS
- CLWYD ROCK
- HEREFORD & THE WYE VALLEY
- HILLWALKING IN SNOWDONIA
- HILLWALKING IN WALES VOL.1
- HILLWALKING IN WALES VOL.2
- LLEYN PENINSULA COASTAL PATH
- WALKING OFFA'S DYKE PATH
- THE PEMBROKESHIRE COASTAL PATH
- THE RIDGES OF SNOWDONIA
- SARN HELEN
- SCRAMBLES IN SNOWDONIA
- SEVERN WALKS
- THE SHROPSHIRE HILLS
- THE SHROPSHIRE WAY
- SPIRIT PATHS OF WALES
- WALKING DOWN THE WYE
- A WELSH COAST TO COAST WALK
- •WELSH WINTER CLIMBS

THE MIDLANDS
- CANAL WALKS VOL 2: MIDLANDS
- THE COTSWOLD WAY
- COTSWOLD WALKS
  BOOK 1: NORTH
  BOOK 2: CENTRAL
  BOOK 3: SOUTH
- THE GRAND UNION CANAL WALK
- HEART OF ENGLAND WALKS
- WALKING IN OXFORDSHIRE
- WALKING IN WARWICKSHIRE
- WALKING IN WORCESTERSHIRE
- WEST MIDLANDS ROCK

SOUTH AND SOUTH-WEST ENGLAND
- WALKING IN BEDFORDSHIRE
- WALKING IN BUCKINGHAMSHIRE
- CHANNEL ISLAND WALKS
- CORNISH ROCK
- WALKING IN CORNWALL
- WALKING IN THE CHILTERNS
- WALKING ON DARTMOOR
- WALKING IN DEVON
- WALKING IN DORSET
- CANAL WALKS VOL 3: SOUTH
- EXMOOR & THE QUANTOCKS
- THE GREATER RIDGEWAY
- WALKING IN HAMPSHIRE
- THE ISLE OF WIGHT
- THE KENNET & AVON WALK
- THE LEA VALLEY WALK
- LONDON: THE DEFINITIVE WALKING GUIDE
- LONDON THEME WALKS
- THE NORTH DOWNS WAY
- THE SOUTH DOWNS WAY
- THE ISLES OF SCILLY
- THE SOUTHERN COAST TO COAST
- SOUTH WEST COAST PATH
- WALKING IN SOMERSET
- WALKING IN SUSSEX
- THE THAMES PATH
- TWO MOORS WAY
- WALKS IN KENT BOOK 1
- WALKS IN KENT BOOK 2
- THE WEALDWAY & VANGUARD WAY

SCOTLAND
- WALKING IN THE ISLE OF ARRAN
- THE BORDER COUNTRY –
  A WALKERS GUIDE
- BORDER COUNTRY CYCLE ROUTES
- BORDER PUBS & INNS –
  A WALKERS' GUIDE
- CAIRNGORMS, WINTER CLIMBS
  5TH EDITION
- CENTRAL HIGHLANDS
  6 LONG DISTANCE WALKS
- WALKING THE GALLOWAY HILLS
- WALKING IN THE HEBRIDES
- NORTH TO THE CAPE
- THE ISLAND OF RHUM

- THE ISLE OF SKYE – A WALKER'S GUIDE
- WALKS IN THE LAMMERMUIRS
- WALKING IN THE LOWTHER HILLS
- THE SCOTTISH GLENS SERIES
  - 1 – CAIRNGORM GLENS
  - 2 – ATHOLL GLENS
  - 3 – GLENS OF RANNOCH
  - 4 – GLENS OF TROSSACH
  - 5 – GLENS OF ARGYLL
  - 6 – THE GREAT GLEN
  - 7 – THE ANGUS GLENS
  - 8 – KNOYDART TO MORVERN
  - 9 – THE GLENS OF ROSS-SHIRE
- SCOTTISH RAILWAY WALKS
- SCRAMBLES IN LOCHABER
- SCRAMBLES IN SKYE
- SKI TOURING IN SCOTLAND
- THE SPEYSIDE WAY
- TORRIDON – A WALKER'S GUIDE
- WALKS FROM THE WEST HIGHLAND RAILWAY
- THE WEST HIGHLAND WAY
- WINTER CLIMBS NEVIS & GLENCOE

IRELAND
- IRISH COASTAL WALKS
- THE IRISH COAST TO COAST
- THE MOUNTAINS OF IRELAND

WALKING AND TREKKING IN THE ALPS
- WALKING IN THE ALPS
- 100 HUT WALKS IN THE ALPS
- CHAMONIX TO ZERMATT
- GRAND TOUR OF MONTE ROSA VOL. 1 AND VOL. 2
- TOUR OF MONT BLANC

FRANCE, BELGIUM AND LUXEMBOURG
- WALKING IN THE ARDENNES
- ROCK CLIMBS BELGIUM & LUX.
- THE BRITTANY COASTAL PATH
- CHAMONIX - MONT BLANC WALKING GUIDE
- WALKING IN THE CEVENNES
- CORSICAN HIGH LEVEL ROUTE: GR20
- THE ECRINS NATIONAL PARK
- WALKING THE FRENCH ALPS: GR5
- WALKING THE FRENCH GORGES
- FRENCH ROCK
- WALKING IN THE HAUTE SAVOIE
- WALKING IN THE LANGUEDOC
- TOUR OF THE OISANS: GR54
- WALKING IN PROVENCE
- THE PYRENEAN TRAIL: GR10
- THE TOUR OF THE QUEYRAS
- ROBERT LOUIS STEVENSON TRAIL
- WALKING IN TARENTAISE & BEAUFORTAIN ALPS
- ROCK CLIMBS IN THE VERDON
- TOUR OF THE VANOISE
- WALKS IN VOLCANO COUNTRY
- SNOWSHOEING MONT BLANC/WESTERN ALPS
- VANOISE SKI TOURING
- ALPINE SKI MOUNTAINEERING
  - VOL 1: WESTERN ALPS
  - VOL 2: EASTERN ALPS

FRANCE/SPAIN
- ROCK CLIMBS IN THE PYRENEES

- WALKS & CLIMBS IN THE PYRENEES
- THE WAY OF ST JAMES VOL 1 AND VOL 2 – WALKER'S
- THE WAY OF ST JAMES LE PUY TO SANTIAGO – CYCLIST'S

SPAIN AND PORTUGAL
- WALKING IN THE ALGARVE
- ANDALUSIAN ROCK CLIMBS
- BIRDWATCHING IN MALLORCA
- COSTA BLANCA ROCK
- COSTA BLANCA WALKS VOL 1
- COSTA BLANCA WALKS VOL 2
- WALKING IN MALLORCA
- ROCK CLIMBS IN MAJORCA, IBIZA & TENERIFE
- WALKING IN MADEIRA
- THE MOUNTAINS OF CENTRAL SPAIN
- THE SPANISH PYRENEES GR11 2ND EDITION
- WALKING IN THE SIERRA NEVADA
- WALKS & CLIMBS IN THE PICOS DE EUROPA
- VIA DE LA PLATA
- WALKING IN THE CANARY ISLANDS VOL 1: WEST AND VOL 2: EAST

SWITZERLAND
- ALPINE PASS ROUTE, SWITZERLAND
- THE BERNESE ALPS A WALKING GUIDE
- CENTRAL SWITZERLAND
- THE JURA: HIGH ROUTE & SKI TRAVERSES
- WALKING IN TICINO, SWITZERLAND
- THE VALAIS, SWITZERLAND – A WALKING GUIDE

GERMANY, AUSTRIA AND EASTERN EUROPE
- MOUNTAIN WALKING IN AUSTRIA
- WALKING IN THE BAVARIAN ALPS
- WALKING IN THE BLACK FOREST
- THE DANUBE CYCLE WAY
- GERMANY'S ROMANTIC ROAD
- WALKING IN THE HARZ MOUNTAINS
- KING LUDWIG WAY
- KLETTERSTEIG NORTHERN LIMESTONE ALPS
- WALKING THE RIVER RHINE TRAIL
- THE MOUNTAINS OF ROMANIA
- WALKING IN THE SALZKAMMERGUT
- HUT-TO-HUT IN THE STUBAI ALPS
- THE HIGH TATRAS
- WALKING IN HUNGARY

SCANDANAVIA
- WALKING IN NORWAY
- ST OLAV'S WAY

ITALY AND SLOVENIA
- ALTA VIA – HIGH LEVEL WALKS DOLOMITES
- CENTRAL APENNINES OF ITALY
- WALKING CENTRAL ITALIAN ALPS
- WALKING IN THE DOLOMITES
- SHORTER WALKS IN THE DOLOMITES
- WALKING ITALY'S GRAN PARADISO
- LONG DISTANCE WALKS IN ITALY'S GRAN PARADISO
- ITALIAN ROCK
- WALKS IN THE JULIAN ALPS
- WALKING IN SICILY

- WALKING IN TUSCANY
- VIA FERRATA SCRAMBLES IN THE DOLOMITES
- VIA FERRATAS OF THE ITALIAN DOLOMITES
  - VOL 1: NORTH, CENTRAL AND EAST
  - VOL 2: SOUTHERN DOLOMITES, BRENTA AND LAKE GARDA

OTHER MEDITERRANEAN COUNTRIES
- THE ATLAS MOUNTAINS
- WALKING IN CYPRUS
- CRETE – THE WHITE MOUNTAINS
- THE MOUNTAINS OF GREECE
- JORDAN – WALKS, TREKS, CAVES ETC.
- THE MOUNTAINS OF TURKEY
- TREKS & CLIMBS WADI RUM JORDAN
- CLIMBS & TREKS IN THE ALA DAG
- WALKING IN PALESTINE

HIMALAYA
- ADVENTURE TREKS IN NEPAL
- ANNAPURNA – A TREKKER'S GUIDE
- EVEREST – A TREKKERS' GUIDE
- GARHWAL & KUMAON – A TREKKER'S GUIDE
- KANGCHENJUNGA – A TREKKER'S GUIDE
- LANGTANG, GOSAINKUND & HELAMBU TREKKERS GUIDE
- MANASLU – A TREKKER'S GUIDE

OTHER COUNTRIES
- MOUNTAIN WALKING IN AFRICA – KENYA
- OZ ROCK – AUSTRALIAN CRAGS
- WALKING IN BRITISH COLUMBIA
- TREKKING IN THE CAUCASUS
- GRAND CANYON & AMERICAN SOUTH WEST
- ROCK CLIMBS IN HONG KONG
- ADVENTURE TREKS WEST NORTH AMERICA
- CLASSIC TRAMPS IN NEW ZEALAND

TECHNIQUES AND EDUCATION
- OUTDOOR PHOTOGRAPHY
- SNOW & ICE TECHNIQUES
- ROPE TECHNIQUES
- THE BOOK OF THE BIVVY
- THE HILLWALKER'S MANUAL
- THE TREKKER'S HANDBOOK
- THE ADVENTURE ALTERNATIVE
- BEYOND ADVENTURE
- FAR HORIZONS – ADVENTURE TRAVEL FOR ALL
- MOUNTAIN WEATHER

Cicerone's mission is to inform and inspire by
providing the best guides to exploring the world

Since its foundation over 30 years ago, Cicerone has specialised in
publishing guidebooks and has built a reputation for quality and reliability.
It now publishes nearly 300 guides to the major destinations for outdoor
enthusiasts, including Europe, UK and the rest of the world.

Written by leading and committed specialists, Cicerone guides are
recognised as the most authoritative. They are full of information, maps and
illustrations so that the user can plan and complete a successful and safe
trip or expedition – be it a long face climb, a walk over Lakeland fells, an
alpine traverse, a Himalayan trek or a ramble in the countryside.

With a thorough introduction to assist planning, clear diagrams, maps and
colour photographs to illustrate the terrain and route, and accurate and
detailed text, Cicerone guides are designed for ease of use and access to
the information.

If the facts on the ground change, or there is any aspect of a guide that you
think we can improve, we are always delighted to hear from you.

Cicerone Press
2 Police Square Milnthorpe Cumbria LA7 7PY
Tel:01539 562 069   Fax:01539 563 417
e-mail:info@cicerone.co.uk   web:www.cicerone.co.uk

CICERONE